The Day Ahead.
The Day Just Passed.

With my thanks to all who freely shared their experience, strength and hope with me - especially my sponsors along the way: Billie B, Sponsor Woman Kathy, Michael and Angelo. Although this format may be unique, the concepts and ideas are not all my own. This is just a tool I use to help me practice these principles in all my affairs.

Take what you need. Feel free to make copies of the meditation sheet if money is tight and you think this will help you practice your program. I only ask you do not reproduce it for your own financial gain, the same as I am sharing it with you... as part of my 12th step. Please note the copyright of all photographs which may not be reproduced, distributed or reused without written permission of copyright holder.

Mark H.

www.TenthStep.com

September 2009

INTRODUCTION

I have found my 10th Step works best when I start my day with just a few minutes of thought, prayer and meditation. By taking ten minutes to look at my day ahead I have something written to look back upon at night when I do my tenth step. It is difficult to deny that any of my character defects arose when it was written in my morning's meditation as an area to look for and act differently.

Some character defects are blatant. They are undeniably wrong. They glare when they appear. Many were done in our past when we were ripping and running. Those are the easy ones to spot.

Unfortunately, as I move ahead one day at a time, my experience has been that most of my character defects are not always so blatant. They are the subtle variety that makes them easy to explain away as justified behaviors.

I believe this is because most of my character defects today are actually my character assets that are normally healthy. But when I take these healthy character assets to excess, they become character defects. The line between the asset and defect are not always easy to spot on casual reflection.

An example is **A**nger. Today I am not a door mat. I am able to stand up for myself and for the things I believe in. When someone tries to take advantage of me, I don't allow it so I don't become angry later on. If a co-worker doesn't do their part of a task, I do not need to just do their work for them. If I do, as time goes on, **A**nger and **R**esentment will build. Then, sooner or later, a situation will arise in which I have a responsibility to give a co-worker part of a task that I should have completed. Instead of recognizing it as **L**aziness on my part, it is much easier to just say, "Well, they never do their job when I need it." So the subtle **A**nger that builds up over time leads me to not acting as a worker among workers. It can lead me to not doing the honest day's work that my employer should expect of me.

So when I know there is a project due and I need a section from Barry, I plan ahead. In the morning meditation, I list Barry under the People, Actions and Institutions as a potential source for character defects of **A**nger and **R**esentment. When at work and Barry hasn't finished his portion, I act with sensitivity and tact without being a doormat. Perhaps I tell Barry I need it by noon, or I will document it in an email to his boss. Then, if noon arrives and it is not done, I do his portion and I also send a sensitive and tactful email to his boss. I do not write that Barry is a lazy slob who refuses to do his work. I can word it to say it appears Barry has too many other priorities that interfered with him completing his part of the project. I just state that to make sure the project was completed on time, I have done Barry's part and ask that we review the distribution of work. The project gets done. I gave Barry the opportunity to do his part. When he didn't, I reacted with sensitivity and tact. When I do my daily 10th step, there is no **A**nger or **R**esentment building up.

Another example is **($)** financial responsibility. Today I don't spend money I do not have. I work for the money I earn. As part of my recovery, I strive to become self supporting by my own contributions. Is this a healthy character asset? I think so.

However, it is easy to take this to extreme. I may not toss in my fair share when the basket comes my way. I may not donate to charities I believe in. I may skimp when it comes to giving gifts to the ones I love. It is very easy to turn my character asset of financial responsibility into the character defect of miserly hoarding my money, or spending money I don't have for material things just make myself appear better than I am.

For example: This publication. I look at the price to be charged. Not all concepts used in the creation of my morning meditation and nightly 10th step are my original idea. Every part of this tool is influenced or derived from material I have read or experiences that others have shared with me. But it would be easy to justify that I should make $5.00 on every copy sold. I worked hard on this and it's a valuable tool that helps keep me sane, serene and sober. But I can't. When I list this against my character defects I see it would be letting my **E**go and **($)** **F**inances/Materialism come into play.

So, not a penny do I earn. This work was done as part of my recovery and the 12th step tells me I must freely share with others what was shared with me

The bottom line for me is if I have written my actions and plans down on paper in the morning, when I do my written 10th step at night I find it harder to explain away those character assets that I have taken to the extreme of becoming a character defect.

So use this tool as you see fit. Adapt it as you need. Look at your day ahead... the people you will interact with, the institutions, and the places you may visit. List them, and follow it with a list of character defects that may arise.

Here is a short example of how I would fill out the meditation sheet:

I look to the day ahead to these People, Actions, or Institutions that I will encounter which may bring up character defects:		
	A	Anger
Publication of journal: **M, SE.**	**R**	Resentment
Barry. Report due. His part not done: **A, R, FRU.**	**SE**	Self-Esteem
Dogs to vet. Heartworm pills & fees, license: **FRU, $$**	**$**	Financial Responsibility
Household chores — Dishes, Vacuum: due: **L, SE & PR**	**D/A**	Dreams and Ambitions
	PR	Personal Relationships
	F	Fear/Frightened
	L	Laziness/Sloth
	M	Materialism
	RT	Retail Therapy
	S/S	Selfish/Self Seeking
	DH	Dishonesty
	D	Depression/Sad
gratitude 1. *Sobriety,* 2. *Family/Friends,* 3. *Home/Pantry,* 4. *Health*	**J/E**	Jealous/Envy
5. *Spouse,* 6. *Job* 7. 8. 9. 10.	**P/E**	Pride/Ego
	Fru	Frustration

Although it may seem like the meditation sheet should be on the right side of the binding, they have been moved to the left so there is a blank page next to it when the book is fully opened. This is done so when reviewing my day and journaling on the blank sheet on the right side of the binding I am able to see my morning meditation on the left side. I have found it helpful to lay it out this way so I don't need to flip back and forth when doing my evening 10th step journaling.

Special orders are always available with extra blank pages, additional character defects or other changes you may find helpful. Let me know how I can be of service to you. Contact me at mark@hawkinsm.com or call me (630)372-2069 and I will do my best to meet your needs.

If you find you like using this journal, order more. If you find this tool helpful, feel free to make copies and use them in your own three ring binder if money is tight. But please do not copy this material for redistribution for your own profit. Also, please note the copyright of all photographs which may not be reproduced, distributed or reused without written permission of copyright holder.

May the God of your understanding bless you as we "trudge the road of happy destiny."

Date: 5/14   **We review our day with the God of our understanding**

Thy will be done, not mine. If we make my will the same as Your will, I will have Serenity & Peace today. Direct my thinking to be divorced from:

▷   Self Pity   ▷   Dishonesty   ▷   Self Seeking Motives   ▷   Unfounded Fears

I ask God that my thoughts do not drift into worry, remorse or morbid reflection.
May all my thoughts and actions today be sensitive & tactful without being servile or scraping.

Into Action   -   Fear of the unknown subsides when action is taken.

In thinking about my day ahead, I may be faced with indecision. I may not be able to determine which course to take.   Here I do not struggle alone. I ask God for:

▷   An inspiration

▷   An intuitive thought or decision, perhaps from his still quiet voice within

▷   I relax and take it easy, not forcing my will

I look to the day ahead to these People, Actions, or Institutions
I will encounter that may bring up character defects:

▷ **A**	Anger
▷ **R**	Resentment
▷ **SE**	Self-Esteem
▷ **$**	Financial Responsibility
▷ **D/A**	Dreams and Ambitions
▷ **PR**	Personal Relationships
▷ **F**	Fear/Frightened
▷ **L**	Laziness/Sloth
▷ **M**	Materialism
▷ **RT**	Retail Therapy
▷ **S/S**	Selfish/Self Seeking
▷ **DH**	Dishonesty
▷ **D**	Depression/Sad
▷ **J/E**	Jealous/Envy
▷ **P/E**	Pride/Ego
▷ **Fru**	Frustration
▷ SP-	

In my Thoughts & Prayers today:

As I finish my morning meditation and start my day, I offer this prayer to the God of my understanding:
Here I am. For better or worse, use me as you will. May I follow the guidance of your still small voice. That voice of reason. That voice of another person or my sponsor. Or the collective voice of a home group. Use my strengths and weaknesses in a way useful to others as well as myself. May I have the strength and the courage to follow that still small voice throughout my day. May I behave with grace, sensitivity, tact, consideration and honesty in all situations I encounter this day.

Finally: I remember when I have no clear guidance from God I must go forward quietly along the path of duty.

At the end of the day (10th Step)**:**
I look back at my actions and thoughts during the day just passed, and ask:

▷   Was I resentful, selfish, dishonest, or afraid in my words and/or actions?

▷   Do I owe anyone an apology?

▷   Have I kept something to myself which should have been discussed with another person at once?

▷   Was I kind and loving toward all?

▷   What could I have done better?

▷   I look at my day to be sure I practiced love and tolerance of others as my code.

▷   I reviewed my day to see that I have ceased fighting anything or anyone.

I then ask God for what corrective measures should be taken.

Date: _____ **We review our day with the God of our understanding**

Thy will be done, not mine. If we make my will the same as Your will, I will have Serenity & Peace today.
Direct my thinking to be divorced from:
   ▷ Self Pity   ▷ Dishonesty   ▷ Self Seeking Motives   ▷ Unfounded Fears
I ask God that my thoughts do not drift into worry, remorse or morbid reflection.
May all my thoughts and actions today be sensitive & tactful without being servile or scraping.

Into Action - Fear of the unknown subsides when action is taken.

In thinking about my day ahead, I may be faced with indecision. I may not be able to determine which course to take. Here I do not struggle alone. I ask God for:
   ▷ An inspiration
   ▷ An intuitive thought or decision, perhaps from his still quiet voice within
   ▷ I relax and take it easy, not forcing my will

I look to the day ahead to these People, Actions, or Institutions
I will encounter that may bring up character defects:

▷	**A**	Anger
▷	**R**	Resentment
▷	**SE**	Self-Esteem
▷	**$**	Financial Responsibility
▷	**D/A**	Dreams and Ambitions
▷	**PR**	Personal Relationships
▷	**F**	Fear/Frightened
▷	**L**	Laziness/Sloth
▷	**M**	Materialism
▷	**RT**	Retail Therapy
▷	**S/S**	Selfish/Self Seeking
▷	**DH**	Dishonesty
▷	**D**	Depression/Sad
▷	**J/E**	Jealous/Envy
▷	**P/E**	Pride/Ego
▷	**Fru**	Frustration

In my Thoughts & Prayers today:

As I finish my morning meditation and start my day, I offer this prayer to the God of my understanding:
   Here I am. For better or worse, use me as you will. May I follow the guidance of your still small voice. That voice of reason. That voice of another person or my sponsor. Or the collective voice of a home group. Use my strengths and weaknesses in a way useful to others as well as myself. May I have the strength and the courage to follow that still small voice throughout my day. May I behave with grace, sensitivity, tact, consideration and honesty in all situations I encounter this day.

Finally: I remember when I have no clear guidance from God I must go forward quietly along the path of duty.

At the end of the day (10th Step):
I look back at my actions and thoughts during the day just passed, and ask:
   ▷ Was I resentful, selfish, dishonest, or afraid in my words and/or actions?
   ▷ Do I owe anyone an apology?
   ▷ Have I kept something to myself which should have been discussed with another person at once?
   ▷ Was I kind and loving toward all?
   ▷ What could I have done better?
   ▷ I look at my day to be sure I practiced love and tolerance of others as my code.
   ▷ I reviewed my day to see that I have ceased fighting anything or anyone.
I then ask God for what corrective measures should be taken.

Date: _____ **We review our day with the God of our understanding**

Thy will be done, not mine. If we make my will the same as Your will, I will have Serenity & Peace today.
Direct my thinking to be divorced from:
  ▷ Self Pity   ▷ Dishonesty   ▷ Self Seeking Motives   ▷ Unfounded Fears
I ask God that my thoughts do not drift into worry, remorse or morbid reflection.
May all my thoughts and actions today be sensitive & tactful without being servile or scraping.

Into Action   -   Fear of the unknown subsides when action is taken.

In thinking about my day ahead, I may be faced with indecision. I may not be able to determine which course to take.   Here I do not struggle alone. I ask God for:
  ▷ An inspiration
  ▷ An intuitive thought or decision, perhaps from his still quiet voice within
  ▷ I relax and take it easy, not forcing my will

I look to the day ahead to these People, Actions, or Institutions
I will encounter that may bring up character defects:

▷	**A**	Anger
▷	**R**	Resentment
▷	**SE**	Self-Esteem
▷	**$**	Financial Responsibility
▷	**D/A**	Dreams and Ambitions
▷	**PR**	Personal Relationships
▷	**F**	Fear/Frightened
▷	**L**	Laziness/Sloth
▷	**M**	Materialism
▷	**RT**	Retail Therapy
▷	**S/S**	Selfish/Self Seeking
▷	**DH**	Dishonesty
▷	**D**	Depression/Sad
▷	**J/E**	Jealous/Envy
▷	**P/E**	Pride/Ego
▷	**Fru**	Frustration

In my Thoughts & Prayers today: _____

As I finish my morning meditation and start my day, I offer this prayer to the God of my understanding:
  Here I am. For better or worse, use me as you will. May I follow the guidance of your still small voice. That voice of reason. That voice of another person or my sponsor. Or the collective voice of a home group. Use my strengths and weaknesses in a way useful to others as well as myself. May I have the strength and the courage to follow that still small voice throughout my day. May I behave with grace, sensitivity, tact, consideration and honesty in all situations I encounter this day.

Finally: I remember when I have no clear guidance from God I must go forward quietly along the path of duty.

At the end of the day (10th Step):
I look back at my actions and thoughts during the day just passed, and ask:
  ▷ Was I resentful, selfish, dishonest, or afraid in my words and/or actions?
  ▷ Do I owe anyone an apology?
  ▷ Have I kept something to myself which should have been discussed with another person at once?
  ▷ Was I kind and loving toward all?
  ▷ What could I have done better?
  ▷ I look at my day to be sure I practiced love and tolerance of others as my code.
  ▷ I reviewed my day to see that I have ceased fighting anything or anyone.
I then ask God for what corrective measures should be taken.

Date: **We review our day with the God of our understanding**

Thy will be done, not mine. If we make my will the same as Your will, I will have Serenity & Peace today. Direct my thinking to be divorced from:

▷   Self Pity   ▷   Dishonesty   ▷   Self Seeking Motives   ▷   Unfounded Fears

I ask God that my thoughts do not drift into worry, remorse or morbid reflection.

May all my thoughts and actions today be sensitive & tactful without being servile or scraping.

Into Action   -   Fear of the unknown subsides when action is taken.

In thinking about my day ahead, I may be faced with indecision. I may not be able to determine which course to take.   Here I do not struggle alone. I ask God for:

> ▷   An inspiration
> ▷   An intuitive thought or decision, perhaps from his still quiet voice within
> ▷   I relax and take it easy, not forcing my will

I look to the day ahead to these People, Actions, or Institutions
I will encounter that may bring up character defects:

▷	**A**	Anger
▷	**R**	Resentment
▷	**SE**	Self-Esteem
▷	**$**	Financial Responsibility
▷	**D/A**	Dreams and Ambitions
▷	**PR**	Personal Relationships
▷	**F**	Fear/Frightened
▷	**L**	Laziness/Sloth
▷	**M**	Materialism
▷	**RT**	Retail Therapy
▷	**S/S**	Selfish/Self Seeking
▷	**DH**	Dishonesty
▷	**D**	Depression/Sad
▷	**J/E**	Jealous/Envy
▷	**P/E**	Pride/Ego
▷	**Fru**	Frustration

In my Thoughts & Prayers today:

As I finish my morning meditation and start my day, I offer this prayer to the God of my understanding:

Here I am. For better or worse, use me as you will. May I follow the guidance of your still small voice. That voice of reason. That voice of another person or my sponsor. Or the collective voice of a home group. Use my strengths and weaknesses in a way useful to others as well as myself. May I have the strength and the courage to follow that still small voice throughout my day. May I behave with grace, sensitivity, tact, consideration and honesty in all situations I encounter this day.

Finally: I remember when I have no clear guidance from God I must go forward quietly along the path of duty.

At the end of the day (10th Step):

I look back at my actions and thoughts during the day just passed, and ask:

> ▷   Was I resentful, selfish, dishonest, or afraid in my words and/or actions?
> ▷   Do I owe anyone an apology?
> ▷   Have I kept something to myself which should have been discussed with another person at once?
> ▷   Was I kind and loving toward all?
> ▷   What could I have done better?
> ▷   I look at my day to be sure I practiced love and tolerance of others as my code.
> ▷   I reviewed my day to see that I have ceased fighting anything or anyone.

I then ask God for what corrective measures should be taken.

Date: _____   **We review our day with the God of our understanding**

Thy will be done, not mine. If we make my will the same as Your will, I will have Serenity & Peace today.
Direct my thinking to be divorced from:

▷ Self Pity   ▷ Dishonesty   ▷ Self Seeking Motives   ▷ Unfounded Fears

I ask God that my thoughts do not drift into worry, remorse or morbid reflection.
May all my thoughts and actions today be sensitive & tactful without being servile or scraping.

Into Action   -   Fear of the unknown subsides when action is taken.

In thinking about my day ahead, I may be faced with indecision. I may not be able to determine which course to take.   Here I do not struggle alone. I ask God for:

▷ An inspiration
▷ An intuitive thought or decision, perhaps from his still quiet voice within
▷ I relax and take it easy, not forcing my will

**I look to the day ahead to these People, Actions, or Institutions
I will encounter that may bring up character defects:**

▷	**A**	Anger
▷	**R**	Resentment
▷	**SE**	Self-Esteem
▷	**$**	Financial Responsibility
▷	**D/A**	Dreams and Ambitions
▷	**PR**	Personal Relationships
▷	**F**	Fear/Frightened
▷	**L**	Laziness/Sloth
▷	**M**	Materialism
▷	**RT**	Retail Therapy
▷	**S/S**	Selfish/Self Seeking
▷	**DH**	Dishonesty
▷	**D**	Depression/Sad
▷	**J/E**	Jealous/Envy
▷	**P/E**	Pride/Ego
▷	**Fru**	Frustration

In my Thoughts & Prayers today: _____

As I finish my morning meditation and start my day, I offer this prayer to the God of my understanding:
Here I am. For better or worse, use me as you will. May I follow the guidance of your still small voice. That voice of reason. That voice of another person or my sponsor. Or the collective voice of a home group. Use my strengths and weaknesses in a way useful to others as well as myself. May I have the strength and the courage to follow that still small voice throughout my day. May I behave with grace, sensitivity, tact, consideration and honesty in all situations I encounter this day.

Finally: I remember when I have no clear guidance from God I must go forward quietly along the path of duty.

At the end of the day (10th Step):
I look back at my actions and thoughts during the day just passed, and ask:

▷ Was I resentful, selfish, dishonest, or afraid in my words and/or actions?
▷ Do I owe anyone an apology?
▷ Have I kept something to myself which should have been discussed with another person at once?
▷ Was I kind and loving toward all?
▷ What could I have done better?
▷ I look at my day to be sure I practiced love and tolerance of others as my code.
▷ I reviewed my day to see that I have ceased fighting anything or anyone.

I then ask God for what corrective measures should be taken.

Date: _____ **We review our day with the God of our understanding**

Thy will be done, not mine. If we make my will the same as Your will, I will have Serenity & Peace today. Direct my thinking to be divorced from:

▷ Self Pity ▷ Dishonesty ▷ Self Seeking Motives ▷ Unfounded Fears

I ask God that my thoughts do not drift into worry, remorse or morbid reflection.

May all my thoughts and actions today be sensitive & tactful without being servile or scraping.

Into Action - Fear of the unknown subsides when action is taken.

In thinking about my day ahead, I may be faced with indecision. I may not be able to determine which course to take. Here I do not struggle alone. I ask God for:

▷ An inspiration
▷ An intuitive thought or decision, perhaps from his still quiet voice within
▷ I relax and take it easy, not forcing my will

I look to the day ahead to these People, Actions, or Institutions I will encounter that may bring up character defects:

▷	**A**	Anger
▷	**R**	Resentment
▷	**SE**	Self-Esteem
▷	**$**	Financial Responsibility
▷	**D/A**	Dreams and Ambitions
▷	**PR**	Personal Relationships
▷	**F**	Fear/Frightened
▷	**L**	Laziness/Sloth
▷	**M**	Materialism
▷	**RT**	Retail Therapy
▷	**S/S**	Selfish/Self Seeking
▷	**DH**	Dishonesty
▷	**D**	Depression/Sad
▷	**J/E**	Jealous/Envy
▷	**P/E**	Pride/Ego
▷	**Fru**	Frustration

In my Thoughts & Prayers today: _____

As I finish my morning meditation and start my day, I offer this prayer to the God of my understanding:

Here I am. For better or worse, use me as you will. May I follow the guidance of your still small voice. That voice of reason. That voice of another person or my sponsor. Or the collective voice of a home group. Use my strengths and weaknesses in a way useful to others as well as myself. May I have the strength and the courage to follow that still small voice throughout my day. May I behave with grace, sensitivity, tact, consideration and honesty in all situations I encounter this day.

Finally: I remember when I have no clear guidance from God I must go forward quietly along the path of duty.

At the end of the day (10th Step):

I look back at my actions and thoughts during the day just passed, and ask:

▷ Was I resentful, selfish, dishonest, or afraid in my words and/or actions?
▷ Do I owe anyone an apology?
▷ Have I kept something to myself which should have been discussed with another person at once?
▷ Was I kind and loving toward all?
▷ What could I have done better?
▷ I look at my day to be sure I practiced love and tolerance of others as my code.
▷ I reviewed my day to see that I have ceased fighting anything or anyone.

I then ask God for what corrective measures should be taken.

Date: _____   **We review our day with the God of our understanding**

Thy will be done, not mine. If we make my will the same as Your will, I will have Serenity & Peace today. Direct my thinking to be divorced from:

▷   Self Pity   ▷   Dishonesty   ▷   Self Seeking Motives   ▷   Unfounded Fears

I ask God that my thoughts do not drift into worry, remorse or morbid reflection.
May all my thoughts and actions today be sensitive & tactful without being servile or scraping.

Into Action   -   Fear of the unknown subsides when action is taken.

In thinking about my day ahead, I may be faced with indecision. I may not be able to determine which course to take.   Here I do not struggle alone. I ask God for:

     ▷   An inspiration
     ▷   An intuitive thought or decision, perhaps from his still quiet voice within
     ▷   I relax and take it easy, not forcing my will

I look to the day ahead to these People, Actions, or Institutions
I will encounter that may bring up character defects:

▷	**A**	Anger
▷	**R**	Resentment
▷	**SE**	Self-Esteem
▷	**$**	Financial Responsibility
▷	**D/A**	Dreams and Ambitions
▷	**PR**	Personal Relationships
▷	**F**	Fear/Frightened
▷	**L**	Laziness/Sloth
▷	**M**	Materialism
▷	**RT**	Retail Therapy
▷	**S/S**	Selfish/Self Seeking
▷	**DH**	Dishonesty
▷	**D**	Depression/Sad
▷	**J/E**	Jealous/Envy
▷	**P/E**	Pride/Ego
▷	**Fru**	Frustration

In my Thoughts & Prayers today: _____

As I finish my morning meditation and start my day, I offer this prayer to the God of my understanding:
Here I am. For better or worse, use me as you will. May I follow the guidance of your still small voice. That voice of reason. That voice of another person or my sponsor. Or the collective voice of a home group. Use my strengths and weaknesses in a way useful to others as well as myself. May I have the strength and the courage to follow that still small voice throughout my day. May I behave with grace, sensitivity, tact, consideration and honesty in all situations I encounter this day.

Finally: I remember when I have no clear guidance from God I must go forward quietly along the path of duty.

At the end of the day (10th Step):
I look back at my actions and thoughts during the day just passed, and ask:

     ▷   Was I resentful, selfish, dishonest, or afraid in my words and/or actions?
     ▷   Do I owe anyone an apology?
     ▷   Have I kept something to myself which should have been discussed with another person at once?
     ▷   Was I kind and loving toward all?
     ▷   What could I have done better?
     ▷   I look at my day to be sure I practiced love and tolerance of others as my code.
     ▷   I reviewed my day to see that I have ceased fighting anything or anyone.

I then ask God for what corrective measures should be taken.

The day ahead... the day just passed.   Date:

Date: _____ **We review our day with the God of our understanding**

Thy will be done, not mine. If we make my will the same as Your will, I will have Serenity & Peace today.
Direct my thinking to be divorced from:
  ▷ Self Pity   ▷ Dishonesty   ▷ Self Seeking Motives   ▷ Unfounded Fears
I ask God that my thoughts do not drift into worry, remorse or morbid reflection.
May all my thoughts and actions today be sensitive & tactful without being servile or scraping.

Into Action   -   Fear of the unknown subsides when action is taken.

In thinking about my day ahead, I may be faced with indecision. I may not be able to determine which course to take.   Here I do not struggle alone. I ask God for:
         ▷ An inspiration
         ▷ An intuitive thought or decision, perhaps from his still quiet voice within
         ▷ I relax and take it easy, not forcing my will

I look to the day ahead to these People, Actions, or Institutions
I will encounter that may bring up character defects:

▷	**A**	Anger
▷	**R**	Resentment
▷	**SE**	Self-Esteem
▷	**$**	Financial Responsibility
▷	**D/A**	Dreams and Ambitions
▷	**PR**	Personal Relationships
▷	**F**	Fear/Frightened
▷	**L**	Laziness/Sloth
▷	**M**	Materialism
▷	**RT**	Retail Therapy
▷	**S/S**	Selfish/Self Seeking
▷	**DH**	Dishonesty
▷	**D**	Depression/Sad
▷	**J/E**	Jealous/Envy
▷	**P/E**	Pride/Ego
▷	**Fru**	Frustration

In my Thoughts & Prayers today: _____

As I finish my morning meditation and start my day, I offer this prayer to the God of my understanding:
    Here I am. For better or worse, use me as you will. May I follow the guidance of your still small voice. That voice of reason. That voice of another person or my sponsor. Or the collective voice of a home group. Use my strengths and weaknesses in a way useful to others as well as myself. May I have the strength and the courage to follow that still small voice throughout my day. May I behave with grace, sensitivity, tact, consideration and honesty in all situations I encounter this day.

Finally: I remember when I have no clear guidance from God I must go forward quietly along the path of duty.

At the end of the day (10th Step)**:**
I look back at my actions and thoughts during the day just passed, and ask:
      ▷ Was I resentful, selfish, dishonest, or afraid in my words and/or actions?
      ▷ Do I owe anyone an apology?
      ▷ Have I kept something to myself which should have been discussed with another person at once?
      ▷ Was I kind and loving toward all?
      ▷ What could I have done better?
      ▷ I look at my day to be sure I practiced love and tolerance of others as my code.
      ▷ I reviewed my day to see that I have ceased fighting anything or anyone.

I then ask God for what corrective measures should be taken.

Date: _____ **We review our day with the God of our understanding**

Thy will be done, not mine. If we make my will the same as Your will, I will have Serenity & Peace today. Direct my thinking to be divorced from:

▷ Self Pity ▷ Dishonesty ▷ Self Seeking Motives ▷ Unfounded Fears

I ask God that my thoughts do not drift into worry, remorse or morbid reflection.

May all my thoughts and actions today be sensitive & tactful without being servile or scraping.

Into Action - Fear of the unknown subsides when action is taken.

In thinking about my day ahead, I may be faced with indecision. I may not be able to determine which course to take. Here I do not struggle alone. I ask God for:

▷ An inspiration
▷ An intuitive thought or decision, perhaps from his still quiet voice within
▷ I relax and take it easy, not forcing my will

I look to the day ahead to these People, Actions, or Institutions
I will encounter that may bring up character defects:

▷	**A**	Anger
▷	**R**	Resentment
▷	**SE**	Self-Esteem
▷	**$**	Financial Responsibility
▷	**D/A**	Dreams and Ambitions
▷	**PR**	Personal Relationships
▷	**F**	Fear/Frightened
▷	**L**	Laziness/Sloth
▷	**M**	Materialism
▷	**RT**	Retail Therapy
▷	**S/S**	Selfish/Self Seeking
▷	**DH**	Dishonesty
▷	**D**	Depression/Sad
▷	**J/E**	Jealous/Envy
▷	**P/E**	Pride/Ego
▷	**Fru**	Frustration

In my Thoughts & Prayers today: _____

As I finish my morning meditation and start my day, I offer this prayer to the God of my understanding:

Here I am. For better or worse, use me as you will. May I follow the guidance of your still small voice. That voice of reason. That voice of another person or my sponsor. Or the collective voice of a home group. Use my strengths and weaknesses in a way useful to others as well as myself. May I have the strength and the courage to follow that still small voice throughout my day. May I behave with grace, sensitivity, tact, consideration and honesty in all situations I encounter this day.

Finally: I remember when I have no clear guidance from God I must go forward quietly along the path of duty.

At the end of the day (10th Step):

I look back at my actions and thoughts during the day just passed, and ask:

▷ Was I resentful, selfish, dishonest, or afraid in my words and/or actions?
▷ Do I owe anyone an apology?
▷ Have I kept something to myself which should have been discussed with another person at once?
▷ Was I kind and loving toward all?
▷ What could I have done better?
▷ I look at my day to be sure I practiced love and tolerance of others as my code.
▷ I reviewed my day to see that I have ceased fighting anything or anyone.

I then ask God for what corrective measures should be taken.

The day ahead... the day just passed.   Date:

Date: _____ **We review our day with the God of our understanding**

Thy will be done, not mine. If we make my will the same as Your will, I will have Serenity & Peace today.
Direct my thinking to be divorced from:

  ▷ Self Pity   ▷ Dishonesty   ▷ Self Seeking Motives   ▷ Unfounded Fears

I ask God that my thoughts do not drift into worry, remorse or morbid reflection.
May all my thoughts and actions today be sensitive & tactful without being servile or scraping.

Into Action   -   Fear of the unknown subsides when action is taken.

In thinking about my day ahead, I may be faced with indecision. I may not be able to determine which course to take. Here I do not struggle alone. I ask God for:

        ▷ An inspiration
        ▷ An intuitive thought or decision, perhaps from his still quiet voice within
        ▷ I relax and take it easy, not forcing my will

I look to the day ahead to these People, Actions, or Institutions
I will encounter that may bring up character defects:

▷	**A**	Anger
▷	**R**	Resentment
▷	**SE**	Self-Esteem
▷	**$**	Financial Responsibility
▷	**D/A**	Dreams and Ambitions
▷	**PR**	Personal Relationships
▷	**F**	Fear/Frightened
▷	**L**	Laziness/Sloth
▷	**M**	Materialism
▷	**RT**	Retail Therapy
▷	**S/S**	Selfish/Self Seeking
▷	**DH**	Dishonesty
▷	**D**	Depression/Sad
▷	**J/E**	Jealous/Envy
▷	**P/E**	Pride/Ego
▷	**Fru**	Frustration

In my Thoughts & Prayers today: _____

As I finish my morning meditation and start my day, I offer this prayer to the God of my understanding:
    Here I am. For better or worse, use me as you will. May I follow the guidance of your still small voice. That voice of reason. That voice of another person or my sponsor. Or the collective voice of a home group. Use my strengths and weaknesses in a way useful to others as well as myself. May I have the strength and the courage to follow that still small voice throughout my day. May I behave with grace, sensitivity, tact, consideration and honesty in all situations I encounter this day.

Finally: I remember when I have no clear guidance from God I must go forward quietly along the path of duty.

At the end of the day (10th Step)**:**
I look back at my actions and thoughts during the day just passed, and ask:

    ▷ Was I resentful, selfish, dishonest, or afraid in my words and/or actions?
    ▷ Do I owe anyone an apology?
    ▷ Have I kept something to myself which should have been discussed with another person at once?
    ▷ Was I kind and loving toward all?
    ▷ What could I have done better?
    ▷ I look at my day to be sure I practiced love and tolerance of others as my code.
    ▷ I reviewed my day to see that I have ceased fighting anything or anyone.

I then ask God for what corrective measures should be taken.

Date: _____ **We review our day with the God of our understanding**

Thy will be done, not mine. If we make my will the same as Your will, I will have Serenity & Peace today.
Direct my thinking to be divorced from:

▷ Self Pity ▷ Dishonesty ▷ Self Seeking Motives ▷ Unfounded Fears

I ask God that my thoughts do not drift into worry, remorse or morbid reflection.
May all my thoughts and actions today be sensitive & tactful without being servile or scraping.

Into Action - Fear of the unknown subsides when action is taken.

In thinking about my day ahead, I may be faced with indecision. I may not be able to determine which course to take. Here I do not struggle alone. I ask God for:

> ▷ An inspiration
> ▷ An intuitive thought or decision, perhaps from his still quiet voice within
> ▷ I relax and take it easy, not forcing my will

I look to the day ahead to these People, Actions, or Institutions
I will encounter that may bring up character defects:

_____
_____
_____
_____
_____
_____
_____
_____
_____
_____
_____
_____

▷	**A**	Anger
▷	**R**	Resentment
▷	**SE**	Self-Esteem
▷	**$**	Financial Responsibility
▷	**D/A**	Dreams and Ambitions
▷	**PR**	Personal Relationships
▷	**F**	Fear/Frightened
▷	**L**	Laziness/Sloth
▷	**M**	Materialism
▷	**RT**	Retail Therapy
▷	**S/S**	Selfish/Self Seeking
▷	**DH**	Dishonesty
▷	**D**	Depression/Sad
▷	**J/E**	Jealous/Envy
▷	**P/E**	Pride/Ego
▷	**Fru**	Frustration

In my Thoughts & Prayers today: _____

As I finish my morning meditation and start my day, I offer this prayer to the God of my understanding:

Here I am. For better or worse, use me as you will. May I follow the guidance of your still small voice. That voice of reason. That voice of another person or my sponsor. Or the collective voice of a home group. Use my strengths and weaknesses in a way useful to others as well as myself. May I have the strength and the courage to follow that still small voice throughout my day. May I behave with grace, sensitivity, tact, consideration and honesty in all situations I encounter this day.

Finally: I remember when I have no clear guidance from God I must go forward quietly along the path of duty.

At the end of the day (10th Step):

I look back at my actions and thoughts during the day just passed, and ask:

> ▷ Was I resentful, selfish, dishonest, or afraid in my words and/or actions?
> ▷ Do I owe anyone an apology?
> ▷ Have I kept something to myself which should have been discussed with another person at once?
> ▷ Was I kind and loving toward all?
> ▷ What could I have done better?
> ▷ I look at my day to be sure I practiced love and tolerance of others as my code.
> ▷ I reviewed my day to see that I have ceased fighting anything or anyone.

I then ask God for what corrective measures should be taken.

The day ahead... the day just passed.   Date:

Date: _____ **We review our day with the God of our understanding**

Thy will be done, not mine. If we make my will the same as Your will, I will have Serenity & Peace today.
Direct my thinking to be divorced from:
 ▷ Self Pity ▷ Dishonesty ▷ Self Seeking Motives ▷ Unfounded Fears
I ask God that my thoughts do not drift into worry, remorse or morbid reflection.
May all my thoughts and actions today be sensitive & tactful without being servile or scraping.

Into Action - Fear of the unknown subsides when action is taken.

In thinking about my day ahead, I may be faced with indecision. I may not be able to determine which course to take. Here I do not struggle alone. I ask God for:
 ▷ An inspiration
 ▷ An intuitive thought or decision, perhaps from his still quiet voice within
 ▷ I relax and take it easy, not forcing my will

**I look to the day ahead to these People, Actions, or Institutions
I will encounter that may bring up character defects:**

▷	**A**	Anger
▷	**R**	Resentment
▷	**SE**	Self-Esteem
▷	**$**	Financial Responsibility
▷	**D/A**	Dreams and Ambitions
▷	**PR**	Personal Relationships
▷	**F**	Fear/Frightened
▷	**L**	Laziness/Sloth
▷	**M**	Materialism
▷	**RT**	Retail Therapy
▷	**S/S**	Selfish/Self Seeking
▷	**DH**	Dishonesty
▷	**D**	Depression/Sad
▷	**J/E**	Jealous/Envy
▷	**P/E**	Pride/Ego
▷	**Fru**	Frustration

In my Thoughts & Prayers today:

As I finish my morning meditation and start my day, I offer this prayer to the God of my understanding:
 Here I am. For better or worse, use me as you will. May I follow the guidance of your still small voice. That voice of reason. That voice of another person or my sponsor. Or the collective voice of a home group. Use my strengths and weaknesses in a way useful to others as well as myself. May I have the strength and the courage to follow that still small voice throughout my day. May I behave with grace, sensitivity, tact, consideration and honesty in all situations I encounter this day.

Finally: I remember when I have no clear guidance from God I must go forward quietly along the path of duty.

At the end of the day (10th Step):
I look back at my actions and thoughts during the day just passed, and ask:
 ▷ Was I resentful, selfish, dishonest, or afraid in my words and/or actions?
 ▷ Do I owe anyone an apology?
 ▷ Have I kept something to myself which should have been discussed with another person at once?
 ▷ Was I kind and loving toward all?
 ▷ What could I have done better?
 ▷ I look at my day to be sure I practiced love and tolerance of others as my code.
 ▷ I reviewed my day to see that I have ceased fighting anything or anyone.
I then ask God for what corrective measures should be taken.

The day ahead... the day just passed.   Date:

Date: _____ **We review our day with the God of our understanding**

Thy will be done, not mine. If we make my will the same as Your will, I will have Serenity & Peace today.
Direct my thinking to be divorced from:
  ▷ Self Pity   ▷ Dishonesty   ▷ Self Seeking Motives   ▷ Unfounded Fears
I ask God that my thoughts do not drift into worry, remorse or morbid reflection.
May all my thoughts and actions today be sensitive & tactful without being servile or scraping.

Into Action   -   Fear of the unknown subsides when action is taken.

In thinking about my day ahead, I may be faced with indecision. I may not be able to determine which course to take.   Here I do not struggle alone. I ask God for:
  ▷ An inspiration
  ▷ An intuitive thought or decision, perhaps from his still quiet voice within
  ▷ I relax and take it easy, not forcing my will

I look to the day ahead to these People, Actions, or Institutions
I will encounter that may bring up character defects:

▷	**A**	Anger
▷	**R**	Resentment
▷	**SE**	Self-Esteem
▷	**$**	Financial Responsibility
▷	**D/A**	Dreams and Ambitions
▷	**PR**	Personal Relationships
▷	**F**	Fear/Frightened
▷	**L**	Laziness/Sloth
▷	**M**	Materialism
▷	**RT**	Retail Therapy
▷	**S/S**	Selfish/Self Seeking
▷	**DH**	Dishonesty
▷	**D**	Depression/Sad
▷	**J/E**	Jealous/Envy
▷	**P/E**	Pride/Ego
▷	**Fru**	Frustration

In my Thoughts & Prayers today: _____

As I finish my morning meditation and start my day, I offer this prayer to the God of my understanding:
   Here I am. For better or worse, use me as you will. May I follow the guidance of your still small voice. That voice of reason. That voice of another person or my sponsor. Or the collective voice of a home group. Use my strengths and weaknesses in a way useful to others as well as myself. May I have the strength and the courage to follow that still small voice throughout my day. May I behave with grace, sensitivity, tact, consideration and honesty in all situations I encounter this day.

Finally: I remember when I have no clear guidance from God I must go forward quietly along the path of duty.

At the end of the day (10th Step)**:**
I look back at my actions and thoughts during the day just passed, and ask:
  ▷ Was I resentful, selfish, dishonest, or afraid in my words and/or actions?
  ▷ Do I owe anyone an apology?
  ▷ Have I kept something to myself which should have been discussed with another person at once?
  ▷ Was I kind and loving toward all?
  ▷ What could I have done better?
  ▷ I look at my day to be sure I practiced love and tolerance of others as my code.
  ▷ I reviewed my day to see that I have ceased fighting anything or anyone.
I then ask God for what corrective measures should be taken.

Date: _____   **We review our day with the God of our understanding**

Thy will be done, not mine. If we make my will the same as Your will, I will have Serenity & Peace today.
Direct my thinking to be divorced from:
  ▷ Self Pity   ▷ Dishonesty   ▷ Self Seeking Motives   ▷ Unfounded Fears
I ask God that my thoughts do not drift into worry, remorse or morbid reflection.
May all my thoughts and actions today be sensitive & tactful without being servile or scraping.

Into Action   -   Fear of the unknown subsides when action is taken.

In thinking about my day ahead, I may be faced with indecision. I may not be able to determine which course to take.   Here I do not struggle alone. I ask God for:
  ▷ An inspiration
  ▷ An intuitive thought or decision, perhaps from his still quiet voice within
  ▷ I relax and take it easy, not forcing my will

**I look to the day ahead to these People, Actions, or Institutions
I will encounter that may bring up character defects:**

▷	**A**	Anger
▷	**R**	Resentment
▷	**SE**	Self-Esteem
▷	**$**	Financial Responsibility
▷	**D/A**	Dreams and Ambitions
▷	**PR**	Personal Relationships
▷	**F**	Fear/Frightened
▷	**L**	Laziness/Sloth
▷	**M**	Materialism
▷	**RT**	Retail Therapy
▷	**S/S**	Selfish/Self Seeking
▷	**DH**	Dishonesty
▷	**D**	Depression/Sad
▷	**J/E**	Jealous/Envy
▷	**P/E**	Pride/Ego
▷	**Fru**	Frustration

In my Thoughts & Prayers today: _____

As I finish my morning meditation and start my day, I offer this prayer to the God of my understanding:
    Here I am. For better or worse, use me as you will. May I follow the guidance of your still small voice. That voice of reason. That voice of another person or my sponsor. Or the collective voice of a home group. Use my strengths and weaknesses in a way useful to others as well as myself. May I have the strength and the courage to follow that still small voice throughout my day. May I behave with grace, sensitivity, tact, consideration and honesty in all situations I encounter this day.

Finally: I remember when I have no clear guidance from God I must go forward quietly along the path of duty.

At the end of the day (10th Step):
I look back at my actions and thoughts during the day just passed, and ask:
  ▷ Was I resentful, selfish, dishonest, or afraid in my words and/or actions?
  ▷ Do I owe anyone an apology?
  ▷ Have I kept something to myself which should have been discussed with another person at once?
  ▷ Was I kind and loving toward all?
  ▷ What could I have done better?
  ▷ I look at my day to be sure I practiced love and tolerance of others as my code.
  ▷ I reviewed my day to see that I have ceased fighting anything or anyone.

I then ask God for what corrective measures should be taken.

The day ahead... the day just passed.   Date:

Date: _____   **We review our day with the God of our understanding**

Thy will be done, not mine. If we make my will the same as Your will, I will have Serenity & Peace today. Direct my thinking to be divorced from:

▷   Self Pity   ▷   Dishonesty   ▷   Self Seeking Motives   ▷   Unfounded Fears

I ask God that my thoughts do not drift into worry, remorse or morbid reflection.

May all my thoughts and actions today be sensitive & tactful without being servile or scraping.

Into Action   -   Fear of the unknown subsides when action is taken.

In thinking about my day ahead, I may be faced with indecision. I may not be able to determine which course to take.   Here I do not struggle alone. I ask God for:

      ▷   An inspiration

      ▷   An intuitive thought or decision, perhaps from his still quiet voice within

      ▷   I relax and take it easy, not forcing my will

I look to the day ahead to these People, Actions, or Institutions
I will encounter that may bring up character defects:

▷	**A**	Anger
▷	**R**	Resentment
▷	**SE**	Self-Esteem
▷	**$**	Financial Responsibility
▷	**D/A**	Dreams and Ambitions
▷	**PR**	Personal Relationships
▷	**F**	Fear/Frightened
▷	**L**	Laziness/Sloth
▷	**M**	Materialism
▷	**RT**	Retail Therapy
▷	**S/S**	Selfish/Self Seeking
▷	**DH**	Dishonesty
▷	**D**	Depression/Sad
▷	**J/E**	Jealous/Envy
▷	**P/E**	Pride/Ego
▷	**Fru**	Frustration

In my Thoughts & Prayers today: _____

As I finish my morning meditation and start my day, I offer this prayer to the God of my understanding:

Here I am. For better or worse, use me as you will. May I follow the guidance of your still small voice. That voice of reason. That voice of another person or my sponsor. Or the collective voice of a home group. Use my strengths and weaknesses in a way useful to others as well as myself. May I have the strength and the courage to follow that still small voice throughout my day. May I behave with grace, sensitivity, tact, consideration and honesty in all situations I encounter this day.

Finally: I remember when I have no clear guidance from God I must go forward quietly along the path of duty.

At the end of the day (10th Step):

I look back at my actions and thoughts during the day just passed, and ask:

      ▷   Was I resentful, selfish, dishonest, or afraid in my words and/or actions?

      ▷   Do I owe anyone an apology?

      ▷   Have I kept something to myself which should have been discussed with another person at once?

      ▷   Was I kind and loving toward all?

      ▷   What could I have done better?

      ▷   I look at my day to be sure I practiced love and tolerance of others as my code.

      ▷   I reviewed my day to see that I have ceased fighting anything or anyone.

I then ask God for what corrective measures should be taken.

The day ahead... the day just passed.   Date:

Date: **We review our day with the God of our understanding**

Thy will be done, not mine. If we make my will the same as Your will, I will have Serenity & Peace today. Direct my thinking to be divorced from:

▷ Self Pity   ▷ Dishonesty   ▷ Self Seeking Motives   ▷ Unfounded Fears

I ask God that my thoughts do not drift into worry, remorse or morbid reflection.

May all my thoughts and actions today be sensitive & tactful without being servile or scraping.

Into Action   -   Fear of the unknown subsides when action is taken.

In thinking about my day ahead, I may be faced with indecision. I may not be able to determine which course to take. Here I do not struggle alone. I ask God for:

       ▷ An inspiration

       ▷ An intuitive thought or decision, perhaps from his still quiet voice within

       ▷ I relax and take it easy, not forcing my will

I look to the day ahead to these People, Actions, or Institutions
I will encounter that may bring up character defects:

▷	**A**	Anger
▷	**R**	Resentment
▷	**SE**	Self-Esteem
▷	**$**	Financial Responsibility
▷	**D/A**	Dreams and Ambitions
▷	**PR**	Personal Relationships
▷	**F**	Fear/Frightened
▷	**L**	Laziness/Sloth
▷	**M**	Materialism
▷	**RT**	Retail Therapy
▷	**S/S**	Selfish/Self Seeking
▷	**DH**	Dishonesty
▷	**D**	Depression/Sad
▷	**J/E**	Jealous/Envy
▷	**P/E**	Pride/Ego
▷	**Fru**	Frustration

In my Thoughts & Prayers today:

As I finish my morning meditation and start my day, I offer this prayer to the God of my understanding:

Here I am. For better or worse, use me as you will. May I follow the guidance of your still small voice. That voice of reason. That voice of another person or my sponsor. Or the collective voice of a home group. Use my strengths and weaknesses in a way useful to others as well as myself. May I have the strength and the courage to follow that still small voice throughout my day. May I behave with grace, sensitivity, tact, consideration and honesty in all situations I encounter this day.

Finally: I remember when I have no clear guidance from God I must go forward quietly along the path of duty.

At the end of the day (10th Step):

I look back at my actions and thoughts during the day just passed, and ask:

       ▷ Was I resentful, selfish, dishonest, or afraid in my words and/or actions?

       ▷ Do I owe anyone an apology?

       ▷ Have I kept something to myself which should have been discussed with another person at once?

       ▷ Was I kind and loving toward all?

       ▷ What could I have done better?

       ▷ I look at my day to be sure I practiced love and tolerance of others as my code.

       ▷ I reviewed my day to see that I have ceased fighting anything or anyone.

I then ask God for what corrective measures should be taken.

The day ahead... the day just passed.   Date:

Date: _____ **We review our day with the God of our understanding**

Thy will be done, not mine. If we make my will the same as Your will, I will have Serenity & Peace today.
Direct my thinking to be divorced from:

▷ Self Pity   ▷ Dishonesty   ▷ Self Seeking Motives   ▷ Unfounded Fears

I ask God that my thoughts do not drift into worry, remorse or morbid reflection.
May all my thoughts and actions today be sensitive & tactful without being servile or scraping.

Into Action   -   Fear of the unknown subsides when action is taken.

In thinking about my day ahead, I may be faced with indecision. I may not be able to determine which course to take.   Here I do not struggle alone. I ask God for:

  ▷ An inspiration
  ▷ An intuitive thought or decision, perhaps from his still quiet voice within
  ▷ I relax and take it easy, not forcing my will

**I look to the day ahead to these People, Actions, or Institutions
I will encounter that may bring up character defects:**

▷	**A**	Anger
▷	**R**	Resentment
▷	**SE**	Self-Esteem
▷	**$**	Financial Responsibility
▷	**D/A**	Dreams and Ambitions
▷	**PR**	Personal Relationships
▷	**F**	Fear/Frightened
▷	**L**	Laziness/Sloth
▷	**M**	Materialism
▷	**RT**	Retail Therapy
▷	**S/S**	Selfish/Self Seeking
▷	**DH**	Dishonesty
▷	**D**	Depression/Sad
▷	**J/E**	Jealous/Envy
▷	**P/E**	Pride/Ego
▷	**Fru**	Frustration

In my Thoughts & Prayers today: _____

As I finish my morning meditation and start my day, I offer this prayer to the God of my understanding:

Here I am. For better or worse, use me as you will. May I follow the guidance of your still small voice. That voice of reason. That voice of another person or my sponsor. Or the collective voice of a home group. Use my strengths and weaknesses in a way useful to others as well as myself. May I have the strength and the courage to follow that still small voice throughout my day. May I behave with grace, sensitivity, tact, consideration and honesty in all situations I encounter this day.

Finally: I remember when I have no clear guidance from God I must go forward quietly along the path of duty.

At the end of the day (10th Step):

I look back at my actions and thoughts during the day just passed, and ask:

  ▷ Was I resentful, selfish, dishonest, or afraid in my words and/or actions?
  ▷ Do I owe anyone an apology?
  ▷ Have I kept something to myself which should have been discussed with another person at once?
  ▷ Was I kind and loving toward all?
  ▷ What could I have done better?
  ▷ I look at my day to be sure I practiced love and tolerance of others as my code.
  ▷ I reviewed my day to see that I have ceased fighting anything or anyone.

I then ask God for what corrective measures should be taken.

Date: _____   **We review our day with the God of our understanding**

Thy will be done, not mine. If we make my will the same as Your will, I will have Serenity & Peace today.
Direct my thinking to be divorced from:

  ▷ Self Pity   ▷ Dishonesty   ▷ Self Seeking Motives   ▷ Unfounded Fears

I ask God that my thoughts do not drift into worry, remorse or morbid reflection.
May all my thoughts and actions today be sensitive & tactful without being servile or scraping.

Into Action   -   Fear of the unknown subsides when action is taken.

In thinking about my day ahead, I may be faced with indecision. I may not be able to determine which course to take.   Here I do not struggle alone. I ask God for:

         ▷ An inspiration
         ▷ An intuitive thought or decision, perhaps from his still quiet voice within
         ▷ I relax and take it easy, not forcing my will

I look to the day ahead to these People, Actions, or Institutions
I will encounter that may bring up character defects:

▷	**A**	Anger
▷	**R**	Resentment
▷	**SE**	Self-Esteem
▷	**$**	Financial Responsibility
▷	**D/A**	Dreams and Ambitions
▷	**PR**	Personal Relationships
▷	**F**	Fear/Frightened
▷	**L**	Laziness/Sloth
▷	**M**	Materialism
▷	**RT**	Retail Therapy
▷	**S/S**	Selfish/Self Seeking
▷	**DH**	Dishonesty
▷	**D**	Depression/Sad
▷	**J/E**	Jealous/Envy
▷	**P/E**	Pride/Ego
▷	**Fru**	Frustration

In my Thoughts & Prayers today: _____

As I finish my morning meditation and start my day, I offer this prayer to the God of my understanding:
Here I am. For better or worse, use me as you will. May I follow the guidance of your still small voice. That voice of reason. That voice of another person or my sponsor. Or the collective voice of a home group. Use my strengths and weaknesses in a way useful to others as well as myself. May I have the strength and the courage to follow that still small voice throughout my day. May I behave with grace, sensitivity, tact, consideration and honesty in all situations I encounter this day.

Finally: I remember when I have no clear guidance from God I must go forward quietly along the path of duty.

At the end of the day (10th Step):
I look back at my actions and thoughts during the day just passed, and ask:

         ▷ Was I resentful, selfish, dishonest, or afraid in my words and/or actions?
         ▷ Do I owe anyone an apology?
         ▷ Have I kept something to myself which should have been discussed with another person at once?
         ▷ Was I kind and loving toward all?
         ▷ What could I have done better?
         ▷ I look at my day to be sure I practiced love and tolerance of others as my code.
         ▷ I reviewed my day to see that I have ceased fighting anything or anyone.

I then ask God for what corrective measures should be taken.

Date: _____ **We review our day with the God of our understanding**

Thy will be done, not mine. If we make my will the same as Your will, I will have Serenity & Peace today. Direct my thinking to be divorced from:

▷ Self Pity ▷ Dishonesty ▷ Self Seeking Motives ▷ Unfounded Fears

I ask God that my thoughts do not drift into worry, remorse or morbid reflection.

May all my thoughts and actions today be sensitive & tactful without being servile or scraping.

Into Action - Fear of the unknown subsides when action is taken.

In thinking about my day ahead, I may be faced with indecision. I may not be able to determine which course to take. Here I do not struggle alone. I ask God for:

▷ An inspiration

▷ An intuitive thought or decision, perhaps from his still quiet voice within

▷ I relax and take it easy, not forcing my will

I look to the day ahead to these People, Actions, or Institutions
I will encounter that may bring up character defects:

▷ **A**	Anger
▷ **R**	Resentment
▷ **SE**	Self-Esteem
▷ **$**	Financial Responsibility
▷ **D/A**	Dreams and Ambitions
▷ **PR**	Personal Relationships
▷ **F**	Fear/Frightened
▷ **L**	Laziness/Sloth
▷ **M**	Materialism
▷ **RT**	Retail Therapy
▷ **S/S**	Selfish/Self Seeking
▷ **DH**	Dishonesty
▷ **D**	Depression/Sad
▷ **J/E**	Jealous/Envy
▷ **P/E**	Pride/Ego
▷ **Fru**	Frustration

In my Thoughts & Prayers today: _____

As I finish my morning meditation and start my day, I offer this prayer to the God of my understanding:

Here I am. For better or worse, use me as you will. May I follow the guidance of your still small voice. That voice of reason. That voice of another person or my sponsor. Or the collective voice of a home group. Use my strengths and weaknesses in a way useful to others as well as myself. May I have the strength and the courage to follow that still small voice throughout my day. May I behave with grace, sensitivity, tact, consideration and honesty in all situations I encounter this day.

Finally: I remember when I have no clear guidance from God I must go forward quietly along the path of duty.

At the end of the day (10th Step):

I look back at my actions and thoughts during the day just passed, and ask:

▷ Was I resentful, selfish, dishonest, or afraid in my words and/or actions?

▷ Do I owe anyone an apology?

▷ Have I kept something to myself which should have been discussed with another person at once?

▷ Was I kind and loving toward all?

▷ What could I have done better?

▷ I look at my day to be sure I practiced love and tolerance of others as my code.

▷ I reviewed my day to see that I have ceased fighting anything or anyone.

I then ask God for what corrective measures should be taken.

The day ahead... the day just passed.   Date:

Date: _____   **We review our day with the God of our understanding**

Thy will be done, not mine. If we make my will the same as Your will, I will have Serenity & Peace today. Direct my thinking to be divorced from:

▷   Self Pity   ▷   Dishonesty   ▷   Self Seeking Motives   ▷   Unfounded Fears

I ask God that my thoughts do not drift into worry, remorse or morbid reflection.

May all my thoughts and actions today be sensitive & tactful without being servile or scraping.

Into Action   -   Fear of the unknown subsides when action is taken.

In thinking about my day ahead, I may be faced with indecision. I may not be able to determine which course to take. Here I do not struggle alone. I ask God for:

        ▷   An inspiration

        ▷   An intuitive thought or decision, perhaps from his still quiet voice within

        ▷   I relax and take it easy, not forcing my will

I look to the day ahead to these People, Actions, or Institutions
I will encounter that may bring up character defects:

▷	**A**	Anger
▷	**R**	Resentment
▷	**SE**	Self-Esteem
▷	**$**	Financial Responsibility
▷	**D/A**	Dreams and Ambitions
▷	**PR**	Personal Relationships
▷	**F**	Fear/Frightened
▷	**L**	Laziness/Sloth
▷	**M**	Materialism
▷	**RT**	Retail Therapy
▷	**S/S**	Selfish/Self Seeking
▷	**DH**	Dishonesty
▷	**D**	Depression/Sad
▷	**J/E**	Jealous/Envy
▷	**P/E**	Pride/Ego
▷	**Fru**	Frustration

In my Thoughts & Prayers today: _____

As I finish my morning meditation and start my day, I offer this prayer to the God of my understanding:

Here I am. For better or worse, use me as you will. May I follow the guidance of your still small voice. That voice of reason. That voice of another person or my sponsor. Or the collective voice of a home group. Use my strengths and weaknesses in a way useful to others as well as myself. May I have the strength and the courage to follow that still small voice throughout my day. May I behave with grace, sensitivity, tact, consideration and honesty in all situations I encounter this day.

Finally: I remember when I have no clear guidance from God I must go forward quietly along the path of duty.

At the end of the day (10th Step):

I look back at my actions and thoughts during the day just passed, and ask:

        ▷   Was I resentful, selfish, dishonest, or afraid in my words and/or actions?

        ▷   Do I owe anyone an apology?

        ▷   Have I kept something to myself which should have been discussed with another person at once?

        ▷   Was I kind and loving toward all?

        ▷   What could I have done better?

        ▷   I look at my day to be sure I practiced love and tolerance of others as my code.

        ▷   I reviewed my day to see that I have ceased fighting anything or anyone.

I then ask God for what corrective measures should be taken.

The day ahead... the day just passed.

Date: _____ **We review our day with the God of our understanding**

Thy will be done, not mine. If we make my will the same as Your will, I will have Serenity & Peace today.
Direct my thinking to be divorced from:

▷ Self Pity ▷ Dishonesty ▷ Self Seeking Motives ▷ Unfounded Fears

I ask God that my thoughts do not drift into worry, remorse or morbid reflection.
May all my thoughts and actions today be sensitive & tactful without being servile or scraping.

Into Action - Fear of the unknown subsides when action is taken.

In thinking about my day ahead, I may be faced with indecision. I may not be able to determine which course to take. Here I do not struggle alone. I ask God for:

▷ An inspiration
▷ An intuitive thought or decision, perhaps from his still quiet voice within
▷ I relax and take it easy, not forcing my will

I look to the day ahead to these People, Actions, or Institutions
I will encounter that may bring up character defects:

▷	**A**	Anger
▷	**R**	Resentment
▷	**SE**	Self-Esteem
▷	**$**	Financial Responsibility
▷	**D/A**	Dreams and Ambitions
▷	**PR**	Personal Relationships
▷	**F**	Fear/Frightened
▷	**L**	Laziness/Sloth
▷	**M**	Materialism
▷	**RT**	Retail Therapy
▷	**S/S**	Selfish/Self Seeking
▷	**DH**	Dishonesty
▷	**D**	Depression/Sad
▷	**J/E**	Jealous/Envy
▷	**P/E**	Pride/Ego
▷	**Fru**	Frustration

In my Thoughts & Prayers today: _____

As I finish my morning meditation and start my day, I offer this prayer to the God of my understanding:

Here I am. For better or worse, use me as you will. May I follow the guidance of your still small voice. That voice of reason. That voice of another person or my sponsor. Or the collective voice of a home group. Use my strengths and weaknesses in a way useful to others as well as myself. May I have the strength and the courage to follow that still small voice throughout my day. May I behave with grace, sensitivity, tact, consideration and honesty in all situations I encounter this day.

Finally: I remember when I have no clear guidance from God I must go forward quietly along the path of duty.

At the end of the day (10th Step):

I look back at my actions and thoughts during the day just passed, and ask:

▷ Was I resentful, selfish, dishonest, or afraid in my words and/or actions?
▷ Do I owe anyone an apology?
▷ Have I kept something to myself which should have been discussed with another person at once?
▷ Was I kind and loving toward all?
▷ What could I have done better?
▷ I look at my day to be sure I practiced love and tolerance of others as my code.
▷ I reviewed my day to see that I have ceased fighting anything or anyone.

I then ask God for what corrective measures should be taken.

The day ahead... the day just passed.   Date:

Date: **We review our day with the God of our understanding**

Thy will be done, not mine. If we make my will the same as Your will, I will have Serenity & Peace today. Direct my thinking to be divorced from:

▷ Self Pity ▷ Dishonesty ▷ Self Seeking Motives ▷ Unfounded Fears

I ask God that my thoughts do not drift into worry, remorse or morbid reflection.

May all my thoughts and actions today be sensitive & tactful without being servile or scraping.

Into Action - Fear of the unknown subsides when action is taken.

In thinking about my day ahead, I may be faced with indecision. I may not be able to determine which course to take. Here I do not struggle alone. I ask God for:

> ▷ An inspiration
> ▷ An intuitive thought or decision, perhaps from his still quiet voice within
> ▷ I relax and take it easy, not forcing my will

**I look to the day ahead to these People, Actions, or Institutions
I will encounter that may bring up character defects:**

▷	**A**	Anger
▷	**R**	Resentment
▷	**SE**	Self-Esteem
▷	**$**	Financial Responsibility
▷	**D/A**	Dreams and Ambitions
▷	**PR**	Personal Relationships
▷	**F**	Fear/Frightened
▷	**L**	Laziness/Sloth
▷	**M**	Materialism
▷	**RT**	Retail Therapy
▷	**S/S**	Selfish/Self Seeking
▷	**DH**	Dishonesty
▷	**D**	Depression/Sad
▷	**J/E**	Jealous/Envy
▷	**P/E**	Pride/Ego
▷	**Fru**	Frustration

In my Thoughts & Prayers today:

As I finish my morning meditation and start my day, I offer this prayer to the God of my understanding:
Here I am. For better or worse, use me as you will. May I follow the guidance of your still small voice. That voice of reason. That voice of another person or my sponsor. Or the collective voice of a home group. Use my strengths and weaknesses in a way useful to others as well as myself. May I have the strength and the courage to follow that still small voice throughout my day. May I behave with grace, sensitivity, tact, consideration and honesty in all situations I encounter this day.

Finally: I remember when I have no clear guidance from God I must go forward quietly along the path of duty.

At the end of the day (10th Step):

I look back at my actions and thoughts during the day just passed, and ask:

> ▷ Was I resentful, selfish, dishonest, or afraid in my words and/or actions?
> ▷ Do I owe anyone an apology?
> ▷ Have I kept something to myself which should have been discussed with another person at once?
> ▷ Was I kind and loving toward all?
> ▷ What could I have done better?
> ▷ I look at my day to be sure I practiced love and tolerance of others as my code.
> ▷ I reviewed my day to see that I have ceased fighting anything or anyone.

I then ask God for what corrective measures should be taken.

Date: _____   **We review our day with the God of our understanding**

Thy will be done, not mine. If we make my will the same as Your will, I will have Serenity & Peace today.
Direct my thinking to be divorced from:
- ▷ Self Pity   ▷ Dishonesty   ▷ Self Seeking Motives   ▷ Unfounded Fears

I ask God that my thoughts do not drift into worry, remorse or morbid reflection.
May all my thoughts and actions today be sensitive & tactful without being servile or scraping.

Into Action   -   Fear of the unknown subsides when action is taken.

In thinking about my day ahead, I may be faced with indecision. I may not be able to determine which course to take.   Here I do not struggle alone. I ask God for:
- ▷ An inspiration
- ▷ An intuitive thought or decision, perhaps from his still quiet voice within
- ▷ I relax and take it easy, not forcing my will

**I look to the day ahead to these People, Actions, or Institutions
I will encounter that may bring up character defects:**

▷	**A**	Anger
▷	**R**	Resentment
▷	**SE**	Self-Esteem
▷	**$**	Financial Responsibility
▷	**D/A**	Dreams and Ambitions
▷	**PR**	Personal Relationships
▷	**F**	Fear/Frightened
▷	**L**	Laziness/Sloth
▷	**M**	Materialism
▷	**RT**	Retail Therapy
▷	**S/S**	Selfish/Self Seeking
▷	**DH**	Dishonesty
▷	**D**	Depression/Sad
▷	**J/E**	Jealous/Envy
▷	**P/E**	Pride/Ego
▷	**Fru**	Frustration

In my Thoughts & Prayers today: _____

As I finish my morning meditation and start my day, I offer this prayer to the God of my understanding:
Here I am. For better or worse, use me as you will. May I follow the guidance of your still small voice. That voice of reason. That voice of another person or my sponsor. Or the collective voice of a home group. Use my strengths and weaknesses in a way useful to others as well as myself. May I have the strength and the courage to follow that still small voice throughout my day. May I behave with grace, sensitivity, tact, consideration and honesty in all situations I encounter this day.

Finally: I remember when I have no clear guidance from God I must go forward quietly along the path of duty.

At the end of the day (10th Step):
I look back at my actions and thoughts during the day just passed, and ask:
- ▷ Was I resentful, selfish, dishonest, or afraid in my words and/or actions?
- ▷ Do I owe anyone an apology?
- ▷ Have I kept something to myself which should have been discussed with another person at once?
- ▷ Was I kind and loving toward all?
- ▷ What could I have done better?
- ▷ I look at my day to be sure I practiced love and tolerance of others as my code.
- ▷ I reviewed my day to see that I have ceased fighting anything or anyone.

I then ask God for what corrective measures should be taken.

Date: _____ **We review our day with the God of our understanding**

Thy will be done, not mine. If we make my will the same as Your will, I will have Serenity & Peace today.
Direct my thinking to be divorced from:

  ▷ Self Pity   ▷ Dishonesty   ▷ Self Seeking Motives   ▷ Unfounded Fears

I ask God that my thoughts do not drift into worry, remorse or morbid reflection.
May all my thoughts and actions today be sensitive & tactful without being servile or scraping.

Into Action   -   Fear of the unknown subsides when action is taken.

In thinking about my day ahead, I may be faced with indecision. I may not be able to determine which course to take. Here I do not struggle alone. I ask God for:

      ▷ An inspiration
      ▷ An intuitive thought or decision, perhaps from his still quiet voice within
      ▷ I relax and take it easy, not forcing my will

**I look to the day ahead to these People, Actions, or Institutions
I will encounter that may bring up character defects:**

▷	**A**	Anger
▷	**R**	Resentment
▷	**SE**	Self-Esteem
▷	**$**	Financial Responsibility
▷	**D/A**	Dreams and Ambitions
▷	**PR**	Personal Relationships
▷	**F**	Fear/Frightened
▷	**L**	Laziness/Sloth
▷	**M**	Materialism
▷	**RT**	Retail Therapy
▷	**S/S**	Selfish/Self Seeking
▷	**DH**	Dishonesty
▷	**D**	Depression/Sad
▷	**J/E**	Jealous/Envy
▷	**P/E**	Pride/Ego
▷	**Fru**	Frustration

In my Thoughts & Prayers today: _____

As I finish my morning meditation and start my day, I offer this prayer to the God of my understanding:

Here I am. For better or worse, use me as you will. May I follow the guidance of your still small voice. That voice of reason. That voice of another person or my sponsor. Or the collective voice of a home group. Use my strengths and weaknesses in a way useful to others as well as myself. May I have the strength and the courage to follow that still small voice throughout my day. May I behave with grace, sensitivity, tact, consideration and honesty in all situations I encounter this day.

Finally: I remember when I have no clear guidance from God I must go forward quietly along the path of duty.

At the end of the day (10th Step):

I look back at my actions and thoughts during the day just passed, and ask:

      ▷ Was I resentful, selfish, dishonest, or afraid in my words and/or actions?
      ▷ Do I owe anyone an apology?
      ▷ Have I kept something to myself which should have been discussed with another person at once?
      ▷ Was I kind and loving toward all?
      ▷ What could I have done better?
      ▷ I look at my day to be sure I practiced love and tolerance of others as my code.
      ▷ I reviewed my day to see that I have ceased fighting anything or anyone.

I then ask God for what corrective measures should be taken.

The day ahead... the day just passed.   Date:

Date: _____ **We review our day with the God of our understanding**

Thy will be done, not mine. If we make my will the same as Your will, I will have Serenity & Peace today.
Direct my thinking to be divorced from:

  ▷ Self Pity   ▷ Dishonesty   ▷ Self Seeking Motives   ▷ Unfounded Fears

I ask God that my thoughts do not drift into worry, remorse or morbid reflection.
May all my thoughts and actions today be sensitive & tactful without being servile or scraping.

Into Action   -   Fear of the unknown subsides when action is taken.

In thinking about my day ahead, I may be faced with indecision. I may not be able to determine which course to take.   Here I do not struggle alone. I ask God for:

      ▷ An inspiration
      ▷ An intuitive thought or decision, perhaps from his still quiet voice within
      ▷ I relax and take it easy, not forcing my will

**I look to the day ahead to these People, Actions, or Institutions
I will encounter that may bring up character defects:**

▷	**A**	Anger
▷	**R**	Resentment
▷	**SE**	Self-Esteem
▷	**$**	Financial Responsibility
▷	**D/A**	Dreams and Ambitions
▷	**PR**	Personal Relationships
▷	**F**	Fear/Frightened
▷	**L**	Laziness/Sloth
▷	**M**	Materialism
▷	**RT**	Retail Therapy
▷	**S/S**	Selfish/Self Seeking
▷	**DH**	Dishonesty
▷	**D**	Depression/Sad
▷	**J/E**	Jealous/Envy
▷	**P/E**	Pride/Ego
▷	**Fru**	Frustration

In my Thoughts & Prayers today: _____

As I finish my morning meditation and start my day, I offer this prayer to the God of my understanding:

Here I am. For better or worse, use me as you will. May I follow the guidance of your still small voice. That voice of reason. That voice of another person or my sponsor. Or the collective voice of a home group. Use my strengths and weaknesses in a way useful to others as well as myself. May I have the strength and the courage to follow that still small voice throughout my day. May I behave with grace, sensitivity, tact, consideration and honesty in all situations I encounter this day.

Finally: I remember when I have no clear guidance from God I must go forward quietly along the path of duty.

At the end of the day (10th Step):

I look back at my actions and thoughts during the day just passed, and ask:

      ▷ Was I resentful, selfish, dishonest, or afraid in my words and/or actions?
      ▷ Do I owe anyone an apology?
      ▷ Have I kept something to myself which should have been discussed with another person at once?
      ▷ Was I kind and loving toward all?
      ▷ What could I have done better?
      ▷ I look at my day to be sure I practiced love and tolerance of others as my code.
      ▷ I reviewed my day to see that I have ceased fighting anything or anyone.

I then ask God for what corrective measures should be taken.

The day ahead... the day just passed.   Date:

Date: _____   **We review our day with the God of our understanding**

Thy will be done, not mine. If we make my will the same as Your will, I will have Serenity & Peace today.
Direct my thinking to be divorced from:

  ▷   Self Pity   ▷   Dishonesty   ▷   Self Seeking Motives   ▷   Unfounded Fears

I ask God that my thoughts do not drift into worry, remorse or morbid reflection.
May all my thoughts and actions today be sensitive & tactful without being servile or scraping.

Into Action   -   Fear of the unknown subsides when action is taken.

In thinking about my day ahead, I may be faced with indecision. I may not be able to determine which course to take.   Here I do not struggle alone. I ask God for:

      ▷   An inspiration
      ▷   An intuitive thought or decision, perhaps from his still quiet voice within
      ▷   I relax and take it easy, not forcing my will

**I look to the day ahead to these People, Actions, or Institutions
I will encounter that may bring up character defects:**

▷	**A**	Anger
▷	**R**	Resentment
▷	**SE**	Self-Esteem
▷	**$**	Financial Responsibility
▷	**D/A**	Dreams and Ambitions
▷	**PR**	Personal Relationships
▷	**F**	Fear/Frightened
▷	**L**	Laziness/Sloth
▷	**M**	Materialism
▷	**RT**	Retail Therapy
▷	**S/S**	Selfish/Self Seeking
▷	**DH**	Dishonesty
▷	**D**	Depression/Sad
▷	**J/E**	Jealous/Envy
▷	**P/E**	Pride/Ego
▷	**Fru**	Frustration

In my Thoughts & Prayers today: _____

As I finish my morning meditation and start my day, I offer this prayer to the God of my understanding:

Here I am. For better or worse, use me as you will. May I follow the guidance of your still small voice. That voice of reason. That voice of another person or my sponsor. Or the collective voice of a home group. Use my strengths and weaknesses in a way useful to others as well as myself. May I have the strength and the courage to follow that still small voice throughout my day. May I behave with grace, sensitivity, tact, consideration and honesty in all situations I encounter this day.

Finally: I remember when I have no clear guidance from God I must go forward quietly along the path of duty.

At the end of the day (10th Step):

I look back at my actions and thoughts during the day just passed, and ask:

      ▷   Was I resentful, selfish, dishonest, or afraid in my words and/or actions?
      ▷   Do I owe anyone an apology?
      ▷   Have I kept something to myself which should have been discussed with another person at once?
      ▷   Was I kind and loving toward all?
      ▷   What could I have done better?
      ▷   I look at my day to be sure I practiced love and tolerance of others as my code.
      ▷   I reviewed my day to see that I have ceased fighting anything or anyone.

I then ask God for what corrective measures should be taken.

The day ahead... the day just passed.   Date:

Date: **We review our day with the God of our understanding**

Thy will be done, not mine. If we make my will the same as Your will, I will have Serenity & Peace today.
Direct my thinking to be divorced from:
- ▷ Self Pity
- ▷ Dishonesty
- ▷ Self Seeking Motives
- ▷ Unfounded Fears

I ask God that my thoughts do not drift into worry, remorse or morbid reflection.
May all my thoughts and actions today be sensitive & tactful without being servile or scraping.

Into Action — Fear of the unknown subsides when action is taken.

In thinking about my day ahead, I may be faced with indecision. I may not be able to determine which course to take. Here I do not struggle alone. I ask God for:
- ▷ An inspiration
- ▷ An intuitive thought or decision, perhaps from his still quiet voice within
- ▷ I relax and take it easy, not forcing my will

I look to the day ahead to these People, Actions, or Institutions
I will encounter that may bring up character defects:

▷	**A**	Anger
▷	**R**	Resentment
▷	**SE**	Self-Esteem
▷	**$**	Financial Responsibility
▷	**D/A**	Dreams and Ambitions
▷	**PR**	Personal Relationships
▷	**F**	Fear/Frightened
▷	**L**	Laziness/Sloth
▷	**M**	Materialism
▷	**RT**	Retail Therapy
▷	**S/S**	Selfish/Self Seeking
▷	**DH**	Dishonesty
▷	**D**	Depression/Sad
▷	**J/E**	Jealous/Envy
▷	**P/E**	Pride/Ego
▷	**Fru**	Frustration

In my Thoughts & Prayers today:

As I finish my morning meditation and start my day, I offer this prayer to the God of my understanding:
Here I am. For better or worse, use me as you will. May I follow the guidance of your still small voice. That voice of reason. That voice of another person or my sponsor. Or the collective voice of a home group. Use my strengths and weaknesses in a way useful to others as well as myself. May I have the strength and the courage to follow that still small voice throughout my day. May I behave with grace, sensitivity, tact, consideration and honesty in all situations I encounter this day.

Finally: I remember when I have no clear guidance from God I must go forward quietly along the path of duty.

At the end of the day (10th Step):
I look back at my actions and thoughts during the day just passed, and ask:
- ▷ Was I resentful, selfish, dishonest, or afraid in my words and/or actions?
- ▷ Do I owe anyone an apology?
- ▷ Have I kept something to myself which should have been discussed with another person at once?
- ▷ Was I kind and loving toward all?
- ▷ What could I have done better?
- ▷ I look at my day to be sure I practiced love and tolerance of others as my code.
- ▷ I reviewed my day to see that I have ceased fighting anything or anyone.

I then ask God for what corrective measures should be taken.

The day ahead... the day just passed.   Date:

Date: **We review our day with the God of our understanding**

Thy will be done, not mine. If we make my will the same as Your will, I will have Serenity & Peace today. Direct my thinking to be divorced from:

▷   Self Pity   ▷   Dishonesty   ▷   Self Seeking Motives   ▷   Unfounded Fears

I ask God that my thoughts do not drift into worry, remorse or morbid reflection.

May all my thoughts and actions today be sensitive & tactful without being servile or scraping.

Into Action   -   Fear of the unknown subsides when action is taken.

In thinking about my day ahead, I may be faced with indecision. I may not be able to determine which course to take.   Here I do not struggle alone. I ask God for:

         ▷   An inspiration

         ▷   An intuitive thought or decision, perhaps from his still quiet voice within

         ▷   I relax and take it easy, not forcing my will

I look to the day ahead to these People, Actions, or Institutions
I will encounter that may bring up character defects:

▷	**A**	Anger
▷	**R**	Resentment
▷	**SE**	Self-Esteem
▷	**$**	Financial Responsibility
▷	**D/A**	Dreams and Ambitions
▷	**PR**	Personal Relationships
▷	**F**	Fear/Frightened
▷	**L**	Laziness/Sloth
▷	**M**	Materialism
▷	**RT**	Retail Therapy
▷	**S/S**	Selfish/Self Seeking
▷	**DH**	Dishonesty
▷	**D**	Depression/Sad
▷	**J/E**	Jealous/Envy
▷	**P/E**	Pride/Ego
▷	**Fru**	Frustration

In my Thoughts & Prayers today:

As I finish my morning meditation and start my day, I offer this prayer to the God of my understanding:

Here I am. For better or worse, use me as you will. May I follow the guidance of your still small voice. That voice of reason. That voice of another person or my sponsor. Or the collective voice of a home group. Use my strengths and weaknesses in a way useful to others as well as myself. May I have the strength and the courage to follow that still small voice throughout my day. May I behave with grace, sensitivity, tact, consideration and honesty in all situations I encounter this day.

Finally: I remember when I have no clear guidance from God I must go forward quietly along the path of duty.

At the end of the day (10th Step):

I look back at my actions and thoughts during the day just passed, and ask:

         ▷   Was I resentful, selfish, dishonest, or afraid in my words and/or actions?

         ▷   Do I owe anyone an apology?

         ▷   Have I kept something to myself which should have been discussed with another person at once?

         ▷   Was I kind and loving toward all?

         ▷   What could I have done better?

         ▷   I look at my day to be sure I practiced love and tolerance of others as my code.

         ▷   I reviewed my day to see that I have ceased fighting anything or anyone.

I then ask God for what corrective measures should be taken.

Date: _____ **We review our day with the God of our understanding**

Thy will be done, not mine. If we make my will the same as Your will, I will have Serenity & Peace today.
Direct my thinking to be divorced from:

  ▷ Self Pity   ▷ Dishonesty   ▷ Self Seeking Motives   ▷ Unfounded Fears

I ask God that my thoughts do not drift into worry, remorse or morbid reflection.
May all my thoughts and actions today be sensitive & tactful without being servile or scraping.

Into Action   -   Fear of the unknown subsides when action is taken.

In thinking about my day ahead, I may be faced with indecision. I may not be able to determine which course to take.   Here I do not struggle alone. I ask God for:

        ▷ An inspiration
        ▷ An intuitive thought or decision, perhaps from his still quiet voice within
        ▷ I relax and take it easy, not forcing my will

**I look to the day ahead to these People, Actions, or Institutions
I will encounter that may bring up character defects:**

▷	**A**	Anger
▷	**R**	Resentment
▷	**SE**	Self-Esteem
▷	**$**	Financial Responsibility
▷	**D/A**	Dreams and Ambitions
▷	**PR**	Personal Relationships
▷	**F**	Fear/Frightened
▷	**L**	Laziness/Sloth
▷	**M**	Materialism
▷	**RT**	Retail Therapy
▷	**S/S**	Selfish/Self Seeking
▷	**DH**	Dishonesty
▷	**D**	Depression/Sad
▷	**J/E**	Jealous/Envy
▷	**P/E**	Pride/Ego
▷	**Fru**	Frustration

In my Thoughts & Prayers today: _____

As I finish my morning meditation and start my day, I offer this prayer to the God of my understanding:

    Here I am. For better or worse, use me as you will. May I follow the guidance of your still small voice. That voice of reason. That voice of another person or my sponsor. Or the collective voice of a home group. Use my strengths and weaknesses in a way useful to others as well as myself. May I have the strength and the courage to follow that still small voice throughout my day. May I behave with grace, sensitivity, tact, consideration and honesty in all situations I encounter this day.

Finally: I remember when I have no clear guidance from God I must go forward quietly along the path of duty.

At the end of the day (10th Step)**:**
I look back at my actions and thoughts during the day just passed, and ask:

    ▷ Was I resentful, selfish, dishonest, or afraid in my words and/or actions?
    ▷ Do I owe anyone an apology?
    ▷ Have I kept something to myself which should have been discussed with another person at once?
    ▷ Was I kind and loving toward all?
    ▷ What could I have done better?
    ▷ I look at my day to be sure I practiced love and tolerance of others as my code.
    ▷ I reviewed my day to see that I have ceased fighting anything or anyone.

I then ask God for what corrective measures should be taken.

The day ahead... the day just passed.   Date:

Date: _____ **We review our day with the God of our understanding**

Thy will be done, not mine. If we make my will the same as Your will, I will have Serenity & Peace today.
Direct my thinking to be divorced from:

▷ Self Pity ▷ Dishonesty ▷ Self Seeking Motives ▷ Unfounded Fears

I ask God that my thoughts do not drift into worry, remorse or morbid reflection.
May all my thoughts and actions today be sensitive & tactful without being servile or scraping.

Into Action - Fear of the unknown subsides when action is taken.

In thinking about my day ahead, I may be faced with indecision. I may not be able to determine which course to take. Here I do not struggle alone. I ask God for:

▷ An inspiration
▷ An intuitive thought or decision, perhaps from his still quiet voice within
▷ I relax and take it easy, not forcing my will

I look to the day ahead to these People, Actions, or Institutions
I will encounter that may bring up character defects:

▷	**A**	Anger
▷	**R**	Resentment
▷	**SE**	Self-Esteem
▷	**$**	Financial Responsibility
▷	**D/A**	Dreams and Ambitions
▷	**PR**	Personal Relationships
▷	**F**	Fear/Frightened
▷	**L**	Laziness/Sloth
▷	**M**	Materialism
▷	**RT**	Retail Therapy
▷	**S/S**	Selfish/Self Seeking
▷	**DH**	Dishonesty
▷	**D**	Depression/Sad
▷	**J/E**	Jealous/Envy
▷	**P/E**	Pride/Ego
▷	**Fru**	Frustration

In my Thoughts & Prayers today: _____

As I finish my morning meditation and start my day, I offer this prayer to the God of my understanding:
Here I am. For better or worse, use me as you will. May I follow the guidance of your still small voice. That voice of reason. That voice of another person or my sponsor. Or the collective voice of a home group. Use my strengths and weaknesses in a way useful to others as well as myself. May I have the strength and the courage to follow that still small voice throughout my day. May I behave with grace, sensitivity, tact, consideration and honesty in all situations I encounter this day.

Finally: I remember when I have no clear guidance from God I must go forward quietly along the path of duty.

At the end of the day (10th Step):

I look back at my actions and thoughts during the day just passed, and ask:

▷ Was I resentful, selfish, dishonest, or afraid in my words and/or actions?
▷ Do I owe anyone an apology?
▷ Have I kept something to myself which should have been discussed with another person at once?
▷ Was I kind and loving toward all?
▷ What could I have done better?
▷ I look at my day to be sure I practiced love and tolerance of others as my code.
▷ I reviewed my day to see that I have ceased fighting anything or anyone.

I then ask God for what corrective measures should be taken.

Date: _____ **We review our day with the God of our understanding**

Thy will be done, not mine. If we make my will the same as Your will, I will have Serenity & Peace today.
Direct my thinking to be divorced from:

▷ Self Pity ▷ Dishonesty ▷ Self Seeking Motives ▷ Unfounded Fears

I ask God that my thoughts do not drift into worry, remorse or morbid reflection.
May all my thoughts and actions today be sensitive & tactful without being servile or scraping.

Into Action - Fear of the unknown subsides when action is taken.

In thinking about my day ahead, I may be faced with indecision. I may not be able to determine which course to take. Here I do not struggle alone. I ask God for:

▷ An inspiration
▷ An intuitive thought or decision, perhaps from his still quiet voice within
▷ I relax and take it easy, not forcing my will

I look to the day ahead to these People, Actions, or Institutions
I will encounter that may bring up character defects:

▷	**A**	Anger
▷	**R**	Resentment
▷	**SE**	Self-Esteem
▷	**$**	Financial Responsibility
▷	**D/A**	Dreams and Ambitions
▷	**PR**	Personal Relationships
▷	**F**	Fear/Frightened
▷	**L**	Laziness/Sloth
▷	**M**	Materialism
▷	**RT**	Retail Therapy
▷	**S/S**	Selfish/Self Seeking
▷	**DH**	Dishonesty
▷	**D**	Depression/Sad
▷	**J/E**	Jealous/Envy
▷	**P/E**	Pride/Ego
▷	**Fru**	Frustration

In my Thoughts & Prayers today: _____

As I finish my morning meditation and start my day, I offer this prayer to the God of my understanding:
Here I am. For better or worse, use me as you will. May I follow the guidance of your still small voice. That voice of reason. That voice of another person or my sponsor. Or the collective voice of a home group. Use my strengths and weaknesses in a way useful to others as well as myself. May I have the strength and the courage to follow that still small voice throughout my day. May I behave with grace, sensitivity, tact, consideration and honesty in all situations I encounter this day.

Finally: I remember when I have no clear guidance from God I must go forward quietly along the path of duty.

At the end of the day (10th Step):

I look back at my actions and thoughts during the day just passed, and ask:

▷ Was I resentful, selfish, dishonest, or afraid in my words and/or actions?
▷ Do I owe anyone an apology?
▷ Have I kept something to myself which should have been discussed with another person at once?
▷ Was I kind and loving toward all?
▷ What could I have done better?
▷ I look at my day to be sure I practiced love and tolerance of others as my code.
▷ I reviewed my day to see that I have ceased fighting anything or anyone.

I then ask God for what corrective measures should be taken.

The day ahead... the day just passed.   Date:

Date: **We review our day with the God of our understanding**

Thy will be done, not mine. If we make my will the same as Your will, I will have Serenity & Peace today. Direct my thinking to be divorced from:

▷ Self Pity   ▷ Dishonesty   ▷ Self Seeking Motives   ▷ Unfounded Fears

I ask God that my thoughts do not drift into worry, remorse or morbid reflection.

May all my thoughts and actions today be sensitive & tactful without being servile or scraping.

Into Action   -   Fear of the unknown subsides when action is taken.

In thinking about my day ahead, I may be faced with indecision. I may not be able to determine which course to take. Here I do not struggle alone. I ask God for:

> ▷ An inspiration
> ▷ An intuitive thought or decision, perhaps from his still quiet voice within
> ▷ I relax and take it easy, not forcing my will

**I look to the day ahead to these People, Actions, or Institutions
I will encounter that may bring up character defects:**

▷	**A**	Anger
▷	**R**	Resentment
▷	**SE**	Self-Esteem
▷	**$**	Financial Responsibility
▷	**D/A**	Dreams and Ambitions
▷	**PR**	Personal Relationships
▷	**F**	Fear/Frightened
▷	**L**	Laziness/Sloth
▷	**M**	Materialism
▷	**RT**	Retail Therapy
▷	**S/S**	Selfish/Self Seeking
▷	**DH**	Dishonesty
▷	**D**	Depression/Sad
▷	**J/E**	Jealous/Envy
▷	**P/E**	Pride/Ego
▷	**Fru**	Frustration

In my Thoughts & Prayers today:

As I finish my morning meditation and start my day, I offer this prayer to the God of my understanding:

Here I am. For better or worse, use me as you will. May I follow the guidance of your still small voice. That voice of reason. That voice of another person or my sponsor. Or the collective voice of a home group. Use my strengths and weaknesses in a way useful to others as well as myself. May I have the strength and the courage to follow that still small voice throughout my day. May I behave with grace, sensitivity, tact, consideration and honesty in all situations I encounter this day.

Finally: I remember when I have no clear guidance from God I must go forward quietly along the path of duty.

At the end of the day (10th Step):

I look back at my actions and thoughts during the day just passed, and ask:

> ▷ Was I resentful, selfish, dishonest, or afraid in my words and/or actions?
> ▷ Do I owe anyone an apology?
> ▷ Have I kept something to myself which should have been discussed with another person at once?
> ▷ Was I kind and loving toward all?
> ▷ What could I have done better?
> ▷ I look at my day to be sure I practiced love and tolerance of others as my code.
> ▷ I reviewed my day to see that I have ceased fighting anything or anyone.

I then ask God for what corrective measures should be taken.

Date: _____ **We review our day with the God of our understanding**

Thy will be done, not mine. If we make my will the same as Your will, I will have Serenity & Peace today.
Direct my thinking to be divorced from:

▷ Self Pity ▷ Dishonesty ▷ Self Seeking Motives ▷ Unfounded Fears

I ask God that my thoughts do not drift into worry, remorse or morbid reflection.
May all my thoughts and actions today be sensitive & tactful without being servile or scraping.

Into Action - Fear of the unknown subsides when action is taken.

In thinking about my day ahead, I may be faced with indecision. I may not be able to determine which course to take. Here I do not struggle alone. I ask God for:

▷ An inspiration
▷ An intuitive thought or decision, perhaps from his still quiet voice within
▷ I relax and take it easy, not forcing my will

**I look to the day ahead to these People, Actions, or Institutions
I will encounter that may bring up character defects:**

_____

_____

_____

_____

_____

_____

_____

_____

_____

_____

_____

_____

▷	**A**	Anger
▷	**R**	Resentment
▷	**SE**	Self-Esteem
▷	**$**	Financial Responsibility
▷	**D/A**	Dreams and Ambitions
▷	**PR**	Personal Relationships
▷	**F**	Fear/Frightened
▷	**L**	Laziness/Sloth
▷	**M**	Materialism
▷	**RT**	Retail Therapy
▷	**S/S**	Selfish/Self Seeking
▷	**DH**	Dishonesty
▷	**D**	Depression/Sad
▷	**J/E**	Jealous/Envy
▷	**P/E**	Pride/Ego
▷	**Fru**	Frustration

In my Thoughts & Prayers today: _____

As I finish my morning meditation and start my day, I offer this prayer to the God of my understanding:
Here I am. For better or worse, use me as you will. May I follow the guidance of your still small voice. That voice of reason. That voice of another person or my sponsor. Or the collective voice of a home group. Use my strengths and weaknesses in a way useful to others as well as myself. May I have the strength and the courage to follow that still small voice throughout my day. May I behave with grace, sensitivity, tact, consideration and honesty in all situations I encounter this day.

Finally: I remember when I have no clear guidance from God I must go forward quietly along the path of duty.

At the end of the day (10th Step):

I look back at my actions and thoughts during the day just passed, and ask:

▷ Was I resentful, selfish, dishonest, or afraid in my words and/or actions?
▷ Do I owe anyone an apology?
▷ Have I kept something to myself which should have been discussed with another person at once?
▷ Was I kind and loving toward all?
▷ What could I have done better?
▷ I look at my day to be sure I practiced love and tolerance of others as my code.
▷ I reviewed my day to see that I have ceased fighting anything or anyone.

I then ask God for what corrective measures should be taken.

The day ahead... the day just passed.   Date:

_____

_____

_____

_____

_____

_____

_____

_____

_____

_____

_____

_____

_____

_____

_____

_____

_____

_____

_____

_____

_____

_____

_____

_____

_____

_____

_____

Date: _____ **We review our day with the God of our understanding**

Thy will be done, not mine. If we make my will the same as Your will, I will have Serenity & Peace today.
Direct my thinking to be divorced from:

  ▷ Self Pity   ▷ Dishonesty   ▷ Self Seeking Motives   ▷ Unfounded Fears

I ask God that my thoughts do not drift into worry, remorse or morbid reflection.
May all my thoughts and actions today be sensitive & tactful without being servile or scraping.

Into Action   -   Fear of the unknown subsides when action is taken.

In thinking about my day ahead, I may be faced with indecision. I may not be able to determine which course to take.   Here I do not struggle alone. I ask God for:

        ▷ An inspiration
        ▷ An intuitive thought or decision, perhaps from his still quiet voice within
        ▷ I relax and take it easy, not forcing my will

**I look to the day ahead to these People, Actions, or Institutions
I will encounter that may bring up character defects:**

▷	**A**	Anger
▷	**R**	Resentment
▷	**SE**	Self-Esteem
▷	**$**	Financial Responsibility
▷	**D/A**	Dreams and Ambitions
▷	**PR**	Personal Relationships
▷	**F**	Fear/Frightened
▷	**L**	Laziness/Sloth
▷	**M**	Materialism
▷	**RT**	Retail Therapy
▷	**S/S**	Selfish/Self Seeking
▷	**DH**	Dishonesty
▷	**D**	Depression/Sad
▷	**J/E**	Jealous/Envy
▷	**P/E**	Pride/Ego
▷	**Fru**	Frustration

In my Thoughts & Prayers today: _____

As I finish my morning meditation and start my day, I offer this prayer to the God of my understanding:
Here I am. For better or worse, use me as you will. May I follow the guidance of your still small voice. That voice of reason. That voice of another person or my sponsor. Or the collective voice of a home group. Use my strengths and weaknesses in a way useful to others as well as myself. May I have the strength and the courage to follow that still small voice throughout my day. May I behave with grace, sensitivity, tact, consideration and honesty in all situations I encounter this day.

Finally: I remember when I have no clear guidance from God I must go forward quietly along the path of duty.

At the end of the day (10th Step):
I look back at my actions and thoughts during the day just passed, and ask:

        ▷ Was I resentful, selfish, dishonest, or afraid in my words and/or actions?
        ▷ Do I owe anyone an apology?
        ▷ Have I kept something to myself which should have been discussed with another person at once?
        ▷ Was I kind and loving toward all?
        ▷ What could I have done better?
        ▷ I look at my day to be sure I practiced love and tolerance of others as my code.
        ▷ I reviewed my day to see that I have ceased fighting anything or anyone.

I then ask God for what corrective measures should be taken.

Date: _____ **We review our day with the God of our understanding**

Thy will be done, not mine. If we make my will the same as Your will, I will have Serenity & Peace today.
Direct my thinking to be divorced from:

▷ Self Pity ▷ Dishonesty ▷ Self Seeking Motives ▷ Unfounded Fears

I ask God that my thoughts do not drift into worry, remorse or morbid reflection.
May all my thoughts and actions today be sensitive & tactful without being servile or scraping.

Into Action - Fear of the unknown subsides when action is taken.

In thinking about my day ahead, I may be faced with indecision. I may not be able to determine which course to take. Here I do not struggle alone. I ask God for:

▷ An inspiration
▷ An intuitive thought or decision, perhaps from his still quiet voice within
▷ I relax and take it easy, not forcing my will

I look to the day ahead to these People, Actions, or Institutions
I will encounter that may bring up character defects:

▷	**A**	Anger
▷	**R**	Resentment
▷	**SE**	Self-Esteem
▷	**$**	Financial Responsibility
▷	**D/A**	Dreams and Ambitions
▷	**PR**	Personal Relationships
▷	**F**	Fear/Frightened
▷	**L**	Laziness/Sloth
▷	**M**	Materialism
▷	**RT**	Retail Therapy
▷	**S/S**	Selfish/Self Seeking
▷	**DH**	Dishonesty
▷	**D**	Depression/Sad
▷	**J/E**	Jealous/Envy
▷	**P/E**	Pride/Ego
▷	**Fru**	Frustration

In my Thoughts & Prayers today: _____

As I finish my morning meditation and start my day, I offer this prayer to the God of my understanding:

Here I am. For better or worse, use me as you will. May I follow the guidance of your still small voice. That voice of reason. That voice of another person or my sponsor. Or the collective voice of a home group. Use my strengths and weaknesses in a way useful to others as well as myself. May I have the strength and the courage to follow that still small voice throughout my day. May I behave with grace, sensitivity, tact, consideration and honesty in all situations I encounter this day.

Finally: I remember when I have no clear guidance from God I must go forward quietly along the path of duty.

At the end of the day (10th Step):

I look back at my actions and thoughts during the day just passed, and ask:

▷ Was I resentful, selfish, dishonest, or afraid in my words and/or actions?
▷ Do I owe anyone an apology?
▷ Have I kept something to myself which should have been discussed with another person at once?
▷ Was I kind and loving toward all?
▷ What could I have done better?
▷ I look at my day to be sure I practiced love and tolerance of others as my code.
▷ I reviewed my day to see that I have ceased fighting anything or anyone.

I then ask God for what corrective measures should be taken.

The day ahead... the day just passed.   Date:

Date: _____ **We review our day with the God of our understanding**

Thy will be done, not mine. If we make my will the same as Your will, I will have Serenity & Peace today. Direct my thinking to be divorced from:

- ▷ Self Pity　　　▷ Dishonesty　　　▷ Self Seeking Motives　　　▷ Unfounded Fears

I ask God that my thoughts do not drift into worry, remorse or morbid reflection.

May all my thoughts and actions today be sensitive & tactful without being servile or scraping.

Into Action - Fear of the unknown subsides when action is taken.

In thinking about my day ahead, I may be faced with indecision. I may not be able to determine which course to take. Here I do not struggle alone. I ask God for:

- ▷ An inspiration
- ▷ An intuitive thought or decision, perhaps from his still quiet voice within
- ▷ I relax and take it easy, not forcing my will

**I look to the day ahead to these People, Actions, or Institutions
I will encounter that may bring up character defects:**

▷	**A**	Anger
▷	**R**	Resentment
▷	**SE**	Self-Esteem
▷	**$**	Financial Responsibility
▷	**D/A**	Dreams and Ambitions
▷	**PR**	Personal Relationships
▷	**F**	Fear/Frightened
▷	**L**	Laziness/Sloth
▷	**M**	Materialism
▷	**RT**	Retail Therapy
▷	**S/S**	Selfish/Self Seeking
▷	**DH**	Dishonesty
▷	**D**	Depression/Sad
▷	**J/E**	Jealous/Envy
▷	**P/E**	Pride/Ego
▷	**Fru**	Frustration

In my Thoughts & Prayers today: _____

As I finish my morning meditation and start my day, I offer this prayer to the God of my understanding:

Here I am. For better or worse, use me as you will. May I follow the guidance of your still small voice. That voice of reason. That voice of another person or my sponsor. Or the collective voice of a home group. Use my strengths and weaknesses in a way useful to others as well as myself. May I have the strength and the courage to follow that still small voice throughout my day. May I behave with grace, sensitivity, tact, consideration and honesty in all situations I encounter this day.

Finally: I remember when I have no clear guidance from God I must go forward quietly along the path of duty.

At the end of the day (10th Step):

I look back at my actions and thoughts during the day just passed, and ask:

- ▷ Was I resentful, selfish, dishonest, or afraid in my words and/or actions?
- ▷ Do I owe anyone an apology?
- ▷ Have I kept something to myself which should have been discussed with another person at once?
- ▷ Was I kind and loving toward all?
- ▷ What could I have done better?
- ▷ I look at my day to be sure I practiced love and tolerance of others as my code.
- ▷ I reviewed my day to see that I have ceased fighting anything or anyone.

I then ask God for what corrective measures should be taken.

The day ahead... the day just passed.
Date:

Date: _____ **We review our day with the God of our understanding**

Thy will be done, not mine. If we make my will the same as Your will, I will have Serenity & Peace today.
Direct my thinking to be divorced from:

  ▷ Self Pity   ▷ Dishonesty   ▷ Self Seeking Motives   ▷ Unfounded Fears

I ask God that my thoughts do not drift into worry, remorse or morbid reflection.
May all my thoughts and actions today be sensitive & tactful without being servile or scraping.

Into Action   -   Fear of the unknown subsides when action is taken.

In thinking about my day ahead, I may be faced with indecision. I may not be able to determine which course to take.   Here I do not struggle alone. I ask God for:

        ▷ An inspiration
        ▷ An intuitive thought or decision, perhaps from his still quiet voice within
        ▷ I relax and take it easy, not forcing my will

**I look to the day ahead to these People, Actions, or Institutions
I will encounter that may bring up character defects:**

▷	**A**	Anger
▷	**R**	Resentment
▷	**SE**	Self-Esteem
▷	**$**	Financial Responsibility
▷	**D/A**	Dreams and Ambitions
▷	**PR**	Personal Relationships
▷	**F**	Fear/Frightened
▷	**L**	Laziness/Sloth
▷	**M**	Materialism
▷	**RT**	Retail Therapy
▷	**S/S**	Selfish/Self Seeking
▷	**DH**	Dishonesty
▷	**D**	Depression/Sad
▷	**J/E**	Jealous/Envy
▷	**P/E**	Pride/Ego
▷	**Fru**	Frustration

In my Thoughts & Prayers today: _____

As I finish my morning meditation and start my day, I offer this prayer to the God of my understanding:
    Here I am. For better or worse, use me as you will. May I follow the guidance of your still small voice. That voice of reason. That voice of another person or my sponsor. Or the collective voice of a home group. Use my strengths and weaknesses in a way useful to others as well as myself. May I have the strength and the courage to follow that still small voice throughout my day. May I behave with grace, sensitivity, tact, consideration and honesty in all situations I encounter this day.

Finally: I remember when I have no clear guidance from God I must go forward quietly along the path of duty.

At the end of the day (10th Step):

I look back at my actions and thoughts during the day just passed, and ask:

      ▷ Was I resentful, selfish, dishonest, or afraid in my words and/or actions?
      ▷ Do I owe anyone an apology?
      ▷ Have I kept something to myself which should have been discussed with another person at once?
      ▷ Was I kind and loving toward all?
      ▷ What could I have done better?
      ▷ I look at my day to be sure I practiced love and tolerance of others as my code.
      ▷ I reviewed my day to see that I have ceased fighting anything or anyone.

I then ask God for what corrective measures should be taken.

The day ahead... the day just passed.   Date:

Date: _____   **We review our day with the God of our understanding**

Thy will be done, not mine. If we make my will the same as Your will, I will have Serenity & Peace today.
Direct my thinking to be divorced from:

▷ Self Pity   ▷ Dishonesty   ▷ Self Seeking Motives   ▷ Unfounded Fears

I ask God that my thoughts do not drift into worry, remorse or morbid reflection.
May all my thoughts and actions today be sensitive & tactful without being servile or scraping.

Into Action   -   Fear of the unknown subsides when action is taken.

In thinking about my day ahead, I may be faced with indecision. I may not be able to determine which course to take.   Here I do not struggle alone. I ask God for:

>   ▷   An inspiration
>   ▷   An intuitive thought or decision, perhaps from his still quiet voice within
>   ▷   I relax and take it easy, not forcing my will

I look to the day ahead to these People, Actions, or Institutions
I will encounter that may bring up character defects:

▷ **A**	Anger
▷ **R**	Resentment
▷ **SE**	Self-Esteem
▷ **$**	Financial Responsibility
▷ **D/A**	Dreams and Ambitions
▷ **PR**	Personal Relationships
▷ **F**	Fear/Frightened
▷ **L**	Laziness/Sloth
▷ **M**	Materialism
▷ **RT**	Retail Therapy
▷ **S/S**	Selfish/Self Seeking
▷ **DH**	Dishonesty
▷ **D**	Depression/Sad
▷ **J/E**	Jealous/Envy
▷ **P/E**	Pride/Ego
▷ **Fru**	Frustration

In my Thoughts & Prayers today: _____

As I finish my morning meditation and start my day, I offer this prayer to the God of my understanding:
Here I am. For better or worse, use me as you will. May I follow the guidance of your still small voice. That voice of reason. That voice of another person or my sponsor. Or the collective voice of a home group. Use my strengths and weaknesses in a way useful to others as well as myself. May I have the strength and the courage to follow that still small voice throughout my day. May I behave with grace, sensitivity, tact, consideration and honesty in all situations I encounter this day.

Finally: I remember when I have no clear guidance from God I must go forward quietly along the path of duty.

At the end of the day (10th Step):

I look back at my actions and thoughts during the day just passed, and ask:

>   ▷   Was I resentful, selfish, dishonest, or afraid in my words and/or actions?
>   ▷   Do I owe anyone an apology?
>   ▷   Have I kept something to myself which should have been discussed with another person at once?
>   ▷   Was I kind and loving toward all?
>   ▷   What could I have done better?
>   ▷   I look at my day to be sure I practiced love and tolerance of others as my code.
>   ▷   I reviewed my day to see that I have ceased fighting anything or anyone.

I then ask God for what corrective measures should be taken.

The day ahead... the day just passed.　　　　Date:

Date: _____ **We review our day with the God of our understanding**

Thy will be done, not mine. If we make my will the same as Your will, I will have Serenity & Peace today.
Direct my thinking to be divorced from:

▷ Self Pity ▷ Dishonesty ▷ Self Seeking Motives ▷ Unfounded Fears

I ask God that my thoughts do not drift into worry, remorse or morbid reflection.
May all my thoughts and actions today be sensitive & tactful without being servile or scraping.

Into Action - Fear of the unknown subsides when action is taken.

In thinking about my day ahead, I may be faced with indecision. I may not be able to determine which course to take. Here I do not struggle alone. I ask God for:

> ▷ An inspiration
> ▷ An intuitive thought or decision, perhaps from his still quiet voice within
> ▷ I relax and take it easy, not forcing my will

I look to the day ahead to these People, Actions, or Institutions
I will encounter that may bring up character defects:

▷	**A**	Anger
▷	**R**	Resentment
▷	**SE**	Self-Esteem
▷	**$**	Financial Responsibility
▷	**D/A**	Dreams and Ambitions
▷	**PR**	Personal Relationships
▷	**F**	Fear/Frightened
▷	**L**	Laziness/Sloth
▷	**M**	Materialism
▷	**RT**	Retail Therapy
▷	**S/S**	Selfish/Self Seeking
▷	**DH**	Dishonesty
▷	**D**	Depression/Sad
▷	**J/E**	Jealous/Envy
▷	**P/E**	Pride/Ego
▷	**Fru**	Frustration

In my Thoughts & Prayers today: _____

As I finish my morning meditation and start my day, I offer this prayer to the God of my understanding:

Here I am. For better or worse, use me as you will. May I follow the guidance of your still small voice. That voice of reason. That voice of another person or my sponsor. Or the collective voice of a home group. Use my strengths and weaknesses in a way useful to others as well as myself. May I have the strength and the courage to follow that still small voice throughout my day. May I behave with grace, sensitivity, tact, consideration and honesty in all situations I encounter this day.

Finally: I remember when I have no clear guidance from God I must go forward quietly along the path of duty.

At the end of the day (10th Step):

I look back at my actions and thoughts during the day just passed, and ask:

> ▷ Was I resentful, selfish, dishonest, or afraid in my words and/or actions?
> ▷ Do I owe anyone an apology?
> ▷ Have I kept something to myself which should have been discussed with another person at once?
> ▷ Was I kind and loving toward all?
> ▷ What could I have done better?
> ▷ I look at my day to be sure I practiced love and tolerance of others as my code.
> ▷ I reviewed my day to see that I have ceased fighting anything or anyone.

I then ask God for what corrective measures should be taken.

The day ahead... the day just passed.   Date:

Date: _____ **We review our day with the God of our understanding**
Thy will be done, not mine. If we make my will the same as Your will, I will have Serenity & Peace today.
Direct my thinking to be divorced from:
  ▷ Self Pity   ▷ Dishonesty   ▷ Self Seeking Motives   ▷ Unfounded Fears
I ask God that my thoughts do not drift into worry, remorse or morbid reflection.
May all my thoughts and actions today be sensitive & tactful without being servile or scraping.

Into Action   -   Fear of the unknown subsides when action is taken.
In thinking about my day ahead, I may be faced with indecision. I may not be able to determine which course to take.   Here I do not struggle alone. I ask God for:
    ▷ An inspiration
    ▷ An intuitive thought or decision, perhaps from his still quiet voice within
    ▷ I relax and take it easy, not forcing my will

**I look to the day ahead to these People, Actions, or Institutions
I will encounter that may bring up character defects:**

▷	**A**	Anger
▷	**R**	Resentment
▷	**SE**	Self-Esteem
▷	**$**	Financial Responsibility
▷	**D/A**	Dreams and Ambitions
▷	**PR**	Personal Relationships
▷	**F**	Fear/Frightened
▷	**L**	Laziness/Sloth
▷	**M**	Materialism
▷	**RT**	Retail Therapy
▷	**S/S**	Selfish/Self Seeking
▷	**DH**	Dishonesty
▷	**D**	Depression/Sad
▷	**J/E**	Jealous/Envy
▷	**P/E**	Pride/Ego
▷	**Fru**	Frustration

In my Thoughts & Prayers today: _____

As I finish my morning meditation and start my day, I offer this prayer to the God of my understanding:
    Here I am. For better or worse, use me as you will. May I follow the guidance of your still small voice. That voice of reason. That voice of another person or my sponsor. Or the collective voice of a home group. Use my strengths and weaknesses in a way useful to others as well as myself. May I have the strength and the courage to follow that still small voice throughout my day. May I behave with grace, sensitivity, tact, consideration and honesty in all situations I encounter this day.

Finally: I remember when I have no clear guidance from God I must go forward quietly along the path of duty.

At the end of the day (10th Step):
I look back at my actions and thoughts during the day just passed, and ask:
    ▷ Was I resentful, selfish, dishonest, or afraid in my words and/or actions?
    ▷ Do I owe anyone an apology?
    ▷ Have I kept something to myself which should have been discussed with another person at once?
    ▷ Was I kind and loving toward all?
    ▷ What could I have done better?
    ▷ I look at my day to be sure I practiced love and tolerance of others as my code.
    ▷ I reviewed my day to see that I have ceased fighting anything or anyone.
I then ask God for what corrective measures should be taken.

The day ahead... the day just passed.   Date:

Date: _____ **We review our day with the God of our understanding**

Thy will be done, not mine. If we make my will the same as Your will, I will have Serenity & Peace today. Direct my thinking to be divorced from:

▷ Self Pity ▷ Dishonesty ▷ Self Seeking Motives ▷ Unfounded Fears

I ask God that my thoughts do not drift into worry, remorse or morbid reflection.
May all my thoughts and actions today be sensitive & tactful without being servile or scraping.

Into Action - Fear of the unknown subsides when action is taken.

In thinking about my day ahead, I may be faced with indecision. I may not be able to determine which course to take. Here I do not struggle alone. I ask God for:

▷ An inspiration
▷ An intuitive thought or decision, perhaps from his still quiet voice within
▷ I relax and take it easy, not forcing my will

**I look to the day ahead to these People, Actions, or Institutions
I will encounter that may bring up character defects:**

▷	**A**	Anger
▷	**R**	Resentment
▷	**SE**	Self-Esteem
▷	**$**	Financial Responsibility
▷	**D/A**	Dreams and Ambitions
▷	**PR**	Personal Relationships
▷	**F**	Fear/Frightened
▷	**L**	Laziness/Sloth
▷	**M**	Materialism
▷	**RT**	Retail Therapy
▷	**S/S**	Selfish/Self Seeking
▷	**DH**	Dishonesty
▷	**D**	Depression/Sad
▷	**J/E**	Jealous/Envy
▷	**P/E**	Pride/Ego
▷	**Fru**	Frustration

In my Thoughts & Prayers today: _____

As I finish my morning meditation and start my day, I offer this prayer to the God of my understanding:

Here I am. For better or worse, use me as you will. May I follow the guidance of your still small voice. That voice of reason. That voice of another person or my sponsor. Or the collective voice of a home group. Use my strengths and weaknesses in a way useful to others as well as myself. May I have the strength and the courage to follow that still small voice throughout my day. May I behave with grace, sensitivity, tact, consideration and honesty in all situations I encounter this day.

Finally: I remember when I have no clear guidance from God I must go forward quietly along the path of duty.

At the end of the day (10th Step):

I look back at my actions and thoughts during the day just passed, and ask:

▷ Was I resentful, selfish, dishonest, or afraid in my words and/or actions?
▷ Do I owe anyone an apology?
▷ Have I kept something to myself which should have been discussed with another person at once?
▷ Was I kind and loving toward all?
▷ What could I have done better?
▷ I look at my day to be sure I practiced love and tolerance of others as my code.
▷ I reviewed my day to see that I have ceased fighting anything or anyone.

I then ask God for what corrective measures should be taken.

The day ahead... the day just passed.   Date:

Date: _____ **We review our day with the God of our understanding**

Thy will be done, not mine. If we make my will the same as Your will, I will have Serenity & Peace today.
Direct my thinking to be divorced from:
  ▷ Self Pity   ▷ Dishonesty   ▷ Self Seeking Motives   ▷ Unfounded Fears
I ask God that my thoughts do not drift into worry, remorse or morbid reflection.
May all my thoughts and actions today be sensitive & tactful without being servile or scraping.

Into Action   -   Fear of the unknown subsides when action is taken.

In thinking about my day ahead, I may be faced with indecision. I may not be able to determine which course to take.   Here I do not struggle alone. I ask God for:
  ▷ An inspiration
  ▷ An intuitive thought or decision, perhaps from his still quiet voice within
  ▷ I relax and take it easy, not forcing my will

I look to the day ahead to these People, Actions, or Institutions
I will encounter that may bring up character defects:

▷	**A**	Anger
▷	**R**	Resentment
▷	**SE**	Self-Esteem
▷	**$**	Financial Responsibility
▷	**D/A**	Dreams and Ambitions
▷	**PR**	Personal Relationships
▷	**F**	Fear/Frightened
▷	**L**	Laziness/Sloth
▷	**M**	Materialism
▷	**RT**	Retail Therapy
▷	**S/S**	Selfish/Self Seeking
▷	**DH**	Dishonesty
▷	**D**	Depression/Sad
▷	**J/E**	Jealous/Envy
▷	**P/E**	Pride/Ego
▷	**Fru**	Frustration

In my Thoughts & Prayers today: _____

As I finish my morning meditation and start my day, I offer this prayer to the God of my understanding:
  Here I am. For better or worse, use me as you will. May I follow the guidance of your still small voice. That voice of reason. That voice of another person or my sponsor. Or the collective voice of a home group. Use my strengths and weaknesses in a way useful to others as well as myself. May I have the strength and the courage to follow that still small voice throughout my day. May I behave with grace, sensitivity, tact, consideration and honesty in all situations I encounter this day.

Finally: I remember when I have no clear guidance from God I must go forward quietly along the path of duty.

At the end of the day (10th Step):
I look back at my actions and thoughts during the day just passed, and ask:
  ▷ Was I resentful, selfish, dishonest, or afraid in my words and/or actions?
  ▷ Do I owe anyone an apology?
  ▷ Have I kept something to myself which should have been discussed with another person at once?
  ▷ Was I kind and loving toward all?
  ▷ What could I have done better?
  ▷ I look at my day to be sure I practiced love and tolerance of others as my code.
  ▷ I reviewed my day to see that I have ceased fighting anything or anyone.
I then ask God for what corrective measures should be taken.

The day ahead... the day just passed.   Date:

Date: _____ **We review our day with the God of our understanding**

Thy will be done, not mine. If we make my will the same as Your will, I will have Serenity & Peace today.
Direct my thinking to be divorced from:

▷ Self Pity ▷ Dishonesty ▷ Self Seeking Motives ▷ Unfounded Fears

I ask God that my thoughts do not drift into worry, remorse or morbid reflection.
May all my thoughts and actions today be sensitive & tactful without being servile or scraping.

Into Action - Fear of the unknown subsides when action is taken.

In thinking about my day ahead, I may be faced with indecision. I may not be able to determine which course to take. Here I do not struggle alone. I ask God for:

▷ An inspiration
▷ An intuitive thought or decision, perhaps from his still quiet voice within
▷ I relax and take it easy, not forcing my will

I look to the day ahead to these People, Actions, or Institutions
I will encounter that may bring up character defects:

▷	**A**	Anger
▷	**R**	Resentment
▷	**SE**	Self-Esteem
▷	**$**	Financial Responsibility
▷	**D/A**	Dreams and Ambitions
▷	**PR**	Personal Relationships
▷	**F**	Fear/Frightened
▷	**L**	Laziness/Sloth
▷	**M**	Materialism
▷	**RT**	Retail Therapy
▷	**S/S**	Selfish/Self Seeking
▷	**DH**	Dishonesty
▷	**D**	Depression/Sad
▷	**J/E**	Jealous/Envy
▷	**P/E**	Pride/Ego
▷	**Fru**	Frustration

In my Thoughts & Prayers today: _____

As I finish my morning meditation and start my day, I offer this prayer to the God of my understanding:

Here I am. For better or worse, use me as you will. May I follow the guidance of your still small voice. That voice of reason. That voice of another person or my sponsor. Or the collective voice of a home group. Use my strengths and weaknesses in a way useful to others as well as myself. May I have the strength and the courage to follow that still small voice throughout my day. May I behave with grace, sensitivity, tact, consideration and honesty in all situations I encounter this day.

Finally: I remember when I have no clear guidance from God I must go forward quietly along the path of duty.

At the end of the day (10th Step):

I look back at my actions and thoughts during the day just passed, and ask:

▷ Was I resentful, selfish, dishonest, or afraid in my words and/or actions?
▷ Do I owe anyone an apology?
▷ Have I kept something to myself which should have been discussed with another person at once?
▷ Was I kind and loving toward all?
▷ What could I have done better?
▷ I look at my day to be sure I practiced love and tolerance of others as my code.
▷ I reviewed my day to see that I have ceased fighting anything or anyone.

I then ask God for what corrective measures should be taken.

Date: _____ **We review our day with the God of our understanding**

Thy will be done, not mine. If we make my will the same as Your will, I will have Serenity & Peace today.
Direct my thinking to be divorced from:

▷ Self Pity ▷ Dishonesty ▷ Self Seeking Motives ▷ Unfounded Fears

I ask God that my thoughts do not drift into worry, remorse or morbid reflection.
May all my thoughts and actions today be sensitive & tactful without being servile or scraping.

Into Action - Fear of the unknown subsides when action is taken.

In thinking about my day ahead, I may be faced with indecision. I may not be able to determine which course to take. Here I do not struggle alone. I ask God for:

▷ An inspiration
▷ An intuitive thought or decision, perhaps from his still quiet voice within
▷ I relax and take it easy, not forcing my will

**I look to the day ahead to these People, Actions, or Institutions
I will encounter that may bring up character defects:**

▷	**A**	Anger
▷	**R**	Resentment
▷	**SE**	Self-Esteem
▷	**$**	Financial Responsibility
▷	**D/A**	Dreams and Ambitions
▷	**PR**	Personal Relationships
▷	**F**	Fear/Frightened
▷	**L**	Laziness/Sloth
▷	**M**	Materialism
▷	**RT**	Retail Therapy
▷	**S/S**	Selfish/Self Seeking
▷	**DH**	Dishonesty
▷	**D**	Depression/Sad
▷	**J/E**	Jealous/Envy
▷	**P/E**	Pride/Ego
▷	**Fru**	Frustration

In my Thoughts & Prayers today: _____

As I finish my morning meditation and start my day, I offer this prayer to the God of my understanding:

Here I am. For better or worse, use me as you will. May I follow the guidance of your still small voice. That voice of reason. That voice of another person or my sponsor. Or the collective voice of a home group. Use my strengths and weaknesses in a way useful to others as well as myself. May I have the strength and the courage to follow that still small voice throughout my day. May I behave with grace, sensitivity, tact, consideration and honesty in all situations I encounter this day.

Finally: I remember when I have no clear guidance from God I must go forward quietly along the path of duty.

At the end of the day (10th Step):

I look back at my actions and thoughts during the day just passed, and ask:

▷ Was I resentful, selfish, dishonest, or afraid in my words and/or actions?
▷ Do I owe anyone an apology?
▷ Have I kept something to myself which should have been discussed with another person at once?
▷ Was I kind and loving toward all?
▷ What could I have done better?
▷ I look at my day to be sure I practiced love and tolerance of others as my code.
▷ I reviewed my day to see that I have ceased fighting anything or anyone.

I then ask God for what corrective measures should be taken.

The day ahead... the day just passed.   Date:

Date: _____ **We review our day with the God of our understanding**

Thy will be done, not mine. If we make my will the same as Your will, I will have Serenity & Peace today.
Direct my thinking to be divorced from:

▷ Self Pity   ▷ Dishonesty   ▷ Self Seeking Motives   ▷ Unfounded Fears

I ask God that my thoughts do not drift into worry, remorse or morbid reflection.
May all my thoughts and actions today be sensitive & tactful without being servile or scraping.

Into Action   -   Fear of the unknown subsides when action is taken.

In thinking about my day ahead, I may be faced with indecision. I may not be able to determine which course to take.   Here I do not struggle alone. I ask God for:

> ▷ An inspiration
> ▷ An intuitive thought or decision, perhaps from his still quiet voice within
> ▷ I relax and take it easy, not forcing my will

**I look to the day ahead to these People, Actions, or Institutions
I will encounter that may bring up character defects:**

_____

_____

_____

_____

_____

_____

_____

_____

_____

_____

_____

_____

▷	**A**	Anger
▷	**R**	Resentment
▷	**SE**	Self-Esteem
▷	**$**	Financial Responsibility
▷	**D/A**	Dreams and Ambitions
▷	**PR**	Personal Relationships
▷	**F**	Fear/Frightened
▷	**L**	Laziness/Sloth
▷	**M**	Materialism
▷	**RT**	Retail Therapy
▷	**S/S**	Selfish/Self Seeking
▷	**DH**	Dishonesty
▷	**D**	Depression/Sad
▷	**J/E**	Jealous/Envy
▷	**P/E**	Pride/Ego
▷	**Fru**	Frustration

In my Thoughts & Prayers today: _____

As I finish my morning meditation and start my day, I offer this prayer to the God of my understanding:
Here I am. For better or worse, use me as you will. May I follow the guidance of your still small voice. That voice of reason. That voice of another person or my sponsor. Or the collective voice of a home group. Use my strengths and weaknesses in a way useful to others as well as myself. May I have the strength and the courage to follow that still small voice throughout my day. May I behave with grace, sensitivity, tact, consideration and honesty in all situations I encounter this day.

Finally: I remember when I have no clear guidance from God I must go forward quietly along the path of duty.

At the end of the day (10th Step):
I look back at my actions and thoughts during the day just passed, and ask:

> ▷ Was I resentful, selfish, dishonest, or afraid in my words and/or actions?
> ▷ Do I owe anyone an apology?
> ▷ Have I kept something to myself which should have been discussed with another person at once?
> ▷ Was I kind and loving toward all?
> ▷ What could I have done better?
> ▷ I look at my day to be sure I practiced love and tolerance of others as my code.
> ▷ I reviewed my day to see that I have ceased fighting anything or anyone.

I then ask God for what corrective measures should be taken.

Date: _____ **We review our day with the God of our understanding**

Thy will be done, not mine. If we make my will the same as Your will, I will have Serenity & Peace today.
Direct my thinking to be divorced from:

> Self Pity   > Dishonesty   > Self Seeking Motives   > Unfounded Fears

I ask God that my thoughts do not drift into worry, remorse or morbid reflection.
May all my thoughts and actions today be sensitive & tactful without being servile or scraping.

Into Action   -   Fear of the unknown subsides when action is taken.

In thinking about my day ahead, I may be faced with indecision. I may not be able to determine which course to take. Here I do not struggle alone. I ask God for:

> An inspiration
> An intuitive thought or decision, perhaps from his still quiet voice within
> I relax and take it easy, not forcing my will

**I look to the day ahead to these People, Actions, or Institutions
I will encounter that may bring up character defects:**

>	**A**	Anger
>	**R**	Resentment
>	**SE**	Self-Esteem
>	**$**	Financial Responsibility
>	**D/A**	Dreams and Ambitions
>	**PR**	Personal Relationships
>	**F**	Fear/Frightened
>	**L**	Laziness/Sloth
>	**M**	Materialism
>	**RT**	Retail Therapy
>	**S/S**	Selfish/Self Seeking
>	**DH**	Dishonesty
>	**D**	Depression/Sad
>	**J/E**	Jealous/Envy
>	**P/E**	Pride/Ego
>	**Fru**	Frustration

In my Thoughts & Prayers today: _____

As I finish my morning meditation and start my day, I offer this prayer to the God of my understanding:

Here I am. For better or worse, use me as you will. May I follow the guidance of your still small voice. That voice of reason. That voice of another person or my sponsor. Or the collective voice of a home group. Use my strengths and weaknesses in a way useful to others as well as myself. May I have the strength and the courage to follow that still small voice throughout my day. May I behave with grace, sensitivity, tact, consideration and honesty in all situations I encounter this day.

Finally: I remember when I have no clear guidance from God I must go forward quietly along the path of duty.

At the end of the day (10th Step):

I look back at my actions and thoughts during the day just passed, and ask:

> Was I resentful, selfish, dishonest, or afraid in my words and/or actions?
> Do I owe anyone an apology?
> Have I kept something to myself which should have been discussed with another person at once?
> Was I kind and loving toward all?
> What could I have done better?
> I look at my day to be sure I practiced love and tolerance of others as my code.
> I reviewed my day to see that I have ceased fighting anything or anyone.

I then ask God for what corrective measures should be taken.

The day ahead... the day just passed.   Date:

Date: _____   **We review our day with the God of our understanding**

Thy will be done, not mine. If we make my will the same as Your will, I will have Serenity & Peace today.
Direct my thinking to be divorced from:

   ▷   Self Pity   ▷   Dishonesty   ▷   Self Seeking Motives   ▷   Unfounded Fears

I ask God that my thoughts do not drift into worry, remorse or morbid reflection.
May all my thoughts and actions today be sensitive & tactful without being servile or scraping.

Into Action   -   Fear of the unknown subsides when action is taken.

In thinking about my day ahead, I may be faced with indecision. I may not be able to determine which course to take.   Here I do not struggle alone. I ask God for:

       ▷   An inspiration
       ▷   An intuitive thought or decision, perhaps from his still quiet voice within
       ▷   I relax and take it easy, not forcing my will

I look to the day ahead to these People, Actions, or Institutions
I will encounter that may bring up character defects:

▷	**A**	Anger
▷	**R**	Resentment
▷	**SE**	Self-Esteem
▷	**$**	Financial Responsibility
▷	**D/A**	Dreams and Ambitions
▷	**PR**	Personal Relationships
▷	**F**	Fear/Frightened
▷	**L**	Laziness/Sloth
▷	**M**	Materialism
▷	**RT**	Retail Therapy
▷	**S/S**	Selfish/Self Seeking
▷	**DH**	Dishonesty
▷	**D**	Depression/Sad
▷	**J/E**	Jealous/Envy
▷	**P/E**	Pride/Ego
▷	**Fru**	Frustration

In my Thoughts & Prayers today: _____

As I finish my morning meditation and start my day, I offer this prayer to the God of my understanding:

Here I am. For better or worse, use me as you will. May I follow the guidance of your still small voice. That voice of reason. That voice of another person or my sponsor. Or the collective voice of a home group. Use my strengths and weaknesses in a way useful to others as well as myself. May I have the strength and the courage to follow that still small voice throughout my day. May I behave with grace, sensitivity, tact, consideration and honesty in all situations I encounter this day.

Finally: I remember when I have no clear guidance from God I must go forward quietly along the path of duty.

At the end of the day (10th Step):

I look back at my actions and thoughts during the day just passed, and ask:

       ▷   Was I resentful, selfish, dishonest, or afraid in my words and/or actions?
       ▷   Do I owe anyone an apology?
       ▷   Have I kept something to myself which should have been discussed with another person at once?
       ▷   Was I kind and loving toward all?
       ▷   What could I have done better?
       ▷   I look at my day to be sure I practiced love and tolerance of others as my code.
       ▷   I reviewed my day to see that I have ceased fighting anything or anyone.

I then ask God for what corrective measures should be taken.

The day ahead... the day just passed.   Date:

Date: _____ **We review our day with the God of our understanding**

Thy will be done, not mine. If we make my will the same as Your will, I will have Serenity & Peace today. Direct my thinking to be divorced from:

▷ Self Pity ▷ Dishonesty ▷ Self Seeking Motives ▷ Unfounded Fears

I ask God that my thoughts do not drift into worry, remorse or morbid reflection.

May all my thoughts and actions today be sensitive & tactful without being servile or scraping.

Into Action - Fear of the unknown subsides when action is taken.

In thinking about my day ahead, I may be faced with indecision. I may not be able to determine which course to take. Here I do not struggle alone. I ask God for:

▷ An inspiration
▷ An intuitive thought or decision, perhaps from his still quiet voice within
▷ I relax and take it easy, not forcing my will

I look to the day ahead to these People, Actions, or Institutions I will encounter that may bring up character defects:

▷	**A**	Anger
▷	**R**	Resentment
▷	**SE**	Self-Esteem
▷	**$**	Financial Responsibility
▷	**D/A**	Dreams and Ambitions
▷	**PR**	Personal Relationships
▷	**F**	Fear/Frightened
▷	**L**	Laziness/Sloth
▷	**M**	Materialism
▷	**RT**	Retail Therapy
▷	**S/S**	Selfish/Self Seeking
▷	**DH**	Dishonesty
▷	**D**	Depression/Sad
▷	**J/E**	Jealous/Envy
▷	**P/E**	Pride/Ego
▷	**Fru**	Frustration

In my Thoughts & Prayers today: _____

As I finish my morning meditation and start my day, I offer this prayer to the God of my understanding:

Here I am. For better or worse, use me as you will. May I follow the guidance of your still small voice. That voice of reason. That voice of another person or my sponsor. Or the collective voice of a home group. Use my strengths and weaknesses in a way useful to others as well as myself. May I have the strength and the courage to follow that still small voice throughout my day. May I behave with grace, sensitivity, tact, consideration and honesty in all situations I encounter this day.

Finally: I remember when I have no clear guidance from God I must go forward quietly along the path of duty.

At the end of the day (10th Step):

I look back at my actions and thoughts during the day just passed, and ask:

▷ Was I resentful, selfish, dishonest, or afraid in my words and/or actions?
▷ Do I owe anyone an apology?
▷ Have I kept something to myself which should have been discussed with another person at once?
▷ Was I kind and loving toward all?
▷ What could I have done better?
▷ I look at my day to be sure I practiced love and tolerance of others as my code.
▷ I reviewed my day to see that I have ceased fighting anything or anyone.

I then ask God for what corrective measures should be taken.

Date: _____ **We review our day with the God of our understanding**

Thy will be done, not mine. If we make my will the same as Your will, I will have Serenity & Peace today.
Direct my thinking to be divorced from:
  ▷ Self Pity   ▷ Dishonesty   ▷ Self Seeking Motives   ▷ Unfounded Fears
I ask God that my thoughts do not drift into worry, remorse or morbid reflection.
May all my thoughts and actions today be sensitive & tactful without being servile or scraping.

Into Action   -   Fear of the unknown subsides when action is taken.

In thinking about my day ahead, I may be faced with indecision. I may not be able to determine which course to take.   Here I do not struggle alone. I ask God for:
        ▷ An inspiration
        ▷ An intuitive thought or decision, perhaps from his still quiet voice within
        ▷ I relax and take it easy, not forcing my will

I look to the day ahead to these People, Actions, or Institutions
I will encounter that may bring up character defects:

▷	**A**	Anger
▷	**R**	Resentment
▷	**SE**	Self-Esteem
▷	**$**	Financial Responsibility
▷	**D/A**	Dreams and Ambitions
▷	**PR**	Personal Relationships
▷	**F**	Fear/Frightened
▷	**L**	Laziness/Sloth
▷	**M**	Materialism
▷	**RT**	Retail Therapy
▷	**S/S**	Selfish/Self Seeking
▷	**DH**	Dishonesty
▷	**D**	Depression/Sad
▷	**J/E**	Jealous/Envy
▷	**P/E**	Pride/Ego
▷	**Fru**	Frustration

In my Thoughts & Prayers today: _____

As I finish my morning meditation and start my day, I offer this prayer to the God of my understanding:
    Here I am. For better or worse, use me as you will. May I follow the guidance of your still small voice. That voice of reason. That voice of another person or my sponsor. Or the collective voice of a home group. Use my strengths and weaknesses in a way useful to others as well as myself. May I have the strength and the courage to follow that still small voice throughout my day. May I behave with grace, sensitivity, tact, consideration and honesty in all situations I encounter this day.

Finally: I remember when I have no clear guidance from God I must go forward quietly along the path of duty.

At the end of the day (10th Step):

I look back at my actions and thoughts during the day just passed, and ask:
     ▷ Was I resentful, selfish, dishonest, or afraid in my words and/or actions?
     ▷ Do I owe anyone an apology?
     ▷ Have I kept something to myself which should have been discussed with another person at once?
     ▷ Was I kind and loving toward all?
     ▷ What could I have done better?
     ▷ I look at my day to be sure I practiced love and tolerance of others as my code.
     ▷ I reviewed my day to see that I have ceased fighting anything or anyone.
I then ask God for what corrective measures should be taken.

The day ahead... the day just passed.   Date:

Date: _____ **We review our day with the God of our understanding**

Thy will be done, not mine. If we make my will the same as Your will, I will have Serenity & Peace today.
Direct my thinking to be divorced from:

  ▷ Self Pity   ▷ Dishonesty   ▷ Self Seeking Motives   ▷ Unfounded Fears

I ask God that my thoughts do not drift into worry, remorse or morbid reflection.
May all my thoughts and actions today be sensitive & tactful without being servile or scraping.

Into Action   -   Fear of the unknown subsides when action is taken.

In thinking about my day ahead, I may be faced with indecision. I may not be able to determine which course to take.   Here I do not struggle alone. I ask God for:

        ▷ An inspiration
        ▷ An intuitive thought or decision, perhaps from his still quiet voice within
        ▷ I relax and take it easy, not forcing my will

I look to the day ahead to these People, Actions, or Institutions
I will encounter that may bring up character defects:

▷	**A**	Anger
▷	**R**	Resentment
▷	**SE**	Self-Esteem
▷	**$**	Financial Responsibility
▷	**D/A**	Dreams and Ambitions
▷	**PR**	Personal Relationships
▷	**F**	Fear/Frightened
▷	**L**	Laziness/Sloth
▷	**M**	Materialism
▷	**RT**	Retail Therapy
▷	**S/S**	Selfish/Self Seeking
▷	**DH**	Dishonesty
▷	**D**	Depression/Sad
▷	**J/E**	Jealous/Envy
▷	**P/E**	Pride/Ego
▷	**Fru**	Frustration

In my Thoughts & Prayers today: _____

As I finish my morning meditation and start my day, I offer this prayer to the God of my understanding:

    Here I am. For better or worse, use me as you will. May I follow the guidance of your still small voice. That voice of reason. That voice of another person or my sponsor. Or the collective voice of a home group. Use my strengths and weaknesses in a way useful to others as well as myself. May I have the strength and the courage to follow that still small voice throughout my day. May I behave with grace, sensitivity, tact, consideration and honesty in all situations I encounter this day.

Finally: I remember when I have no clear guidance from God I must go forward quietly along the path of duty.

At the end of the day (10th Step):

I look back at my actions and thoughts during the day just passed, and ask:

      ▷ Was I resentful, selfish, dishonest, or afraid in my words and/or actions?
      ▷ Do I owe anyone an apology?
      ▷ Have I kept something to myself which should have been discussed with another person at once?
      ▷ Was I kind and loving toward all?
      ▷ What could I have done better?
      ▷ I look at my day to be sure I practiced love and tolerance of others as my code.
      ▷ I reviewed my day to see that I have ceased fighting anything or anyone.

I then ask God for what corrective measures should be taken.

Date: _____ **We review our day with the God of our understanding**

Thy will be done, not mine. If we make my will the same as Your will, I will have Serenity & Peace today.
Direct my thinking to be divorced from:
  ▷ Self Pity   ▷ Dishonesty   ▷ Self Seeking Motives   ▷ Unfounded Fears
I ask God that my thoughts do not drift into worry, remorse or morbid reflection.
May all my thoughts and actions today be sensitive & tactful without being servile or scraping.

Into Action   -   Fear of the unknown subsides when action is taken.

In thinking about my day ahead, I may be faced with indecision. I may not be able to determine which course to take.   Here I do not struggle alone. I ask God for:
  ▷ An inspiration
  ▷ An intuitive thought or decision, perhaps from his still quiet voice within
  ▷ I relax and take it easy, not forcing my will

**I look to the day ahead to these People, Actions, or Institutions
I will encounter that may bring up character defects:**

▷	**A**	Anger
▷	**R**	Resentment
▷	**SE**	Self-Esteem
▷	**$**	Financial Responsibility
▷	**D/A**	Dreams and Ambitions
▷	**PR**	Personal Relationships
▷	**F**	Fear/Frightened
▷	**L**	Laziness/Sloth
▷	**M**	Materialism
▷	**RT**	Retail Therapy
▷	**S/S**	Selfish/Self Seeking
▷	**DH**	Dishonesty
▷	**D**	Depression/Sad
▷	**J/E**	Jealous/Envy
▷	**P/E**	Pride/Ego
▷	**Fru**	Frustration

In my Thoughts & Prayers today: _____

As I finish my morning meditation and start my day, I offer this prayer to the God of my understanding:
  Here I am. For better or worse, use me as you will. May I follow the guidance of your still small voice. That voice of reason. That voice of another person or my sponsor. Or the collective voice of a home group. Use my strengths and weaknesses in a way useful to others as well as myself. May I have the strength and the courage to follow that still small voice throughout my day. May I behave with grace, sensitivity, tact, consideration and honesty in all situations I encounter this day.

Finally: I remember when I have no clear guidance from God I must go forward quietly along the path of duty.

At the end of the day (10th Step):
I look back at my actions and thoughts during the day just passed, and ask:
  ▷ Was I resentful, selfish, dishonest, or afraid in my words and/or actions?
  ▷ Do I owe anyone an apology?
  ▷ Have I kept something to myself which should have been discussed with another person at once?
  ▷ Was I kind and loving toward all?
  ▷ What could I have done better?
  ▷ I look at my day to be sure I practiced love and tolerance of others as my code.
  ▷ I reviewed my day to see that I have ceased fighting anything or anyone.
I then ask God for what corrective measures should be taken.

The day ahead... the day just passed.   Date:

Date: _____ **We review our day with the God of our understanding**

Thy will be done, not mine. If we make my will the same as Your will, I will have Serenity & Peace today.
Direct my thinking to be divorced from:
▷ Self Pity   ▷ Dishonesty   ▷ Self Seeking Motives   ▷ Unfounded Fears
I ask God that my thoughts do not drift into worry, remorse or morbid reflection.
May all my thoughts and actions today be sensitive & tactful without being servile or scraping.

Into Action   -   Fear of the unknown subsides when action is taken.

In thinking about my day ahead, I may be faced with indecision. I may not be able to determine which course to take.   Here I do not struggle alone. I ask God for:
> ▷ An inspiration
> ▷ An intuitive thought or decision, perhaps from his still quiet voice within
> ▷ I relax and take it easy, not forcing my will

I look to the day ahead to these People, Actions, or Institutions
I will encounter that may bring up character defects:

▷	**A**	Anger
▷	**R**	Resentment
▷	**SE**	Self-Esteem
▷	**$**	Financial Responsibility
▷	**D/A**	Dreams and Ambitions
▷	**PR**	Personal Relationships
▷	**F**	Fear/Frightened
▷	**L**	Laziness/Sloth
▷	**M**	Materialism
▷	**RT**	Retail Therapy
▷	**S/S**	Selfish/Self Seeking
▷	**DH**	Dishonesty
▷	**D**	Depression/Sad
▷	**J/E**	Jealous/Envy
▷	**P/E**	Pride/Ego
▷	**Fru**	Frustration

In my Thoughts & Prayers today: _____

As I finish my morning meditation and start my day, I offer this prayer to the God of my understanding:
Here I am. For better or worse, use me as you will. May I follow the guidance of your still small voice. That voice of reason. That voice of another person or my sponsor. Or the collective voice of a home group. Use my strengths and weaknesses in a way useful to others as well as myself. May I have the strength and the courage to follow that still small voice throughout my day. May I behave with grace, sensitivity, tact, consideration and honesty in all situations I encounter this day.

Finally: I remember when I have no clear guidance from God I must go forward quietly along the path of duty.

At the end of the day (10th Step):
I look back at my actions and thoughts during the day just passed, and ask:
> ▷ Was I resentful, selfish, dishonest, or afraid in my words and/or actions?
> ▷ Do I owe anyone an apology?
> ▷ Have I kept something to myself which should have been discussed with another person at once?
> ▷ Was I kind and loving toward all?
> ▷ What could I have done better?
> ▷ I look at my day to be sure I practiced love and tolerance of others as my code.
> ▷ I reviewed my day to see that I have ceased fighting anything or anyone.

I then ask God for what corrective measures should be taken.

Date: _____ **We review our day with the God of our understanding**

Thy will be done, not mine. If we make my will the same as Your will, I will have Serenity & Peace today.
Direct my thinking to be divorced from:

   ▷ Self Pity   ▷ Dishonesty   ▷ Self Seeking Motives   ▷ Unfounded Fears

I ask God that my thoughts do not drift into worry, remorse or morbid reflection.
May all my thoughts and actions today be sensitive & tactful without being servile or scraping.

Into Action   -   Fear of the unknown subsides when action is taken.

In thinking about my day ahead, I may be faced with indecision. I may not be able to determine which course to take.   Here I do not struggle alone. I ask God for:

       ▷ An inspiration
       ▷ An intuitive thought or decision, perhaps from his still quiet voice within
       ▷ I relax and take it easy, not forcing my will

I look to the day ahead to these People, Actions, or Institutions
I will encounter that may bring up character defects:

▷	**A**	Anger
▷	**R**	Resentment
▷	**SE**	Self-Esteem
▷	**$**	Financial Responsibility
▷	**D/A**	Dreams and Ambitions
▷	**PR**	Personal Relationships
▷	**F**	Fear/Frightened
▷	**L**	Laziness/Sloth
▷	**M**	Materialism
▷	**RT**	Retail Therapy
▷	**S/S**	Selfish/Self Seeking
▷	**DH**	Dishonesty
▷	**D**	Depression/Sad
▷	**J/E**	Jealous/Envy
▷	**P/E**	Pride/Ego
▷	**Fru**	Frustration

In my Thoughts & Prayers today: _____

As I finish my morning meditation and start my day, I offer this prayer to the God of my understanding:

    Here I am. For better or worse, use me as you will. May I follow the guidance of your still small voice. That voice of reason. That voice of another person or my sponsor. Or the collective voice of a home group. Use my strengths and weaknesses in a way useful to others as well as myself. May I have the strength and the courage to follow that still small voice throughout my day. May I behave with grace, sensitivity, tact, consideration and honesty in all situations I encounter this day.

Finally: I remember when I have no clear guidance from God I must go forward quietly along the path of duty.

At the end of the day (10th Step):

I look back at my actions and thoughts during the day just passed, and ask:

     ▷ Was I resentful, selfish, dishonest, or afraid in my words and/or actions?
     ▷ Do I owe anyone an apology?
     ▷ Have I kept something to myself which should have been discussed with another person at once?
     ▷ Was I kind and loving toward all?
     ▷ What could I have done better?
     ▷ I look at my day to be sure I practiced love and tolerance of others as my code.
     ▷ I reviewed my day to see that I have ceased fighting anything or anyone.

I then ask God for what corrective measures should be taken.

The day ahead... the day just passed.　　　　Date:

Date: _____ **We review our day with the God of our understanding**

Thy will be done, not mine. If we make my will the same as Your will, I will have Serenity & Peace today.
Direct my thinking to be divorced from:

▷ Self Pity ▷ Dishonesty ▷ Self Seeking Motives ▷ Unfounded Fears

I ask God that my thoughts do not drift into worry, remorse or morbid reflection.
May all my thoughts and actions today be sensitive & tactful without being servile or scraping.

Into Action - Fear of the unknown subsides when action is taken.

In thinking about my day ahead, I may be faced with indecision. I may not be able to determine which course to take. Here I do not struggle alone. I ask God for:

▷ An inspiration
▷ An intuitive thought or decision, perhaps from his still quiet voice within
▷ I relax and take it easy, not forcing my will

**I look to the day ahead to these People, Actions, or Institutions
I will encounter that may bring up character defects:**

▷	**A**	Anger
▷	**R**	Resentment
▷	**SE**	Self-Esteem
▷	**$**	Financial Responsibility
▷	**D/A**	Dreams and Ambitions
▷	**PR**	Personal Relationships
▷	**F**	Fear/Frightened
▷	**L**	Laziness/Sloth
▷	**M**	Materialism
▷	**RT**	Retail Therapy
▷	**S/S**	Selfish/Self Seeking
▷	**DH**	Dishonesty
▷	**D**	Depression/Sad
▷	**J/E**	Jealous/Envy
▷	**P/E**	Pride/Ego
▷	**Fru**	Frustration

In my Thoughts & Prayers today: _____

As I finish my morning meditation and start my day, I offer this prayer to the God of my understanding:

Here I am. For better or worse, use me as you will. May I follow the guidance of your still small voice. That voice of reason. That voice of another person or my sponsor. Or the collective voice of a home group. Use my strengths and weaknesses in a way useful to others as well as myself. May I have the strength and the courage to follow that still small voice throughout my day. May I behave with grace, sensitivity, tact, consideration and honesty in all situations I encounter this day.

Finally: I remember when I have no clear guidance from God I must go forward quietly along the path of duty.

At the end of the day (10th Step):

I look back at my actions and thoughts during the day just passed, and ask:

▷ Was I resentful, selfish, dishonest, or afraid in my words and/or actions?
▷ Do I owe anyone an apology?
▷ Have I kept something to myself which should have been discussed with another person at once?
▷ Was I kind and loving toward all?
▷ What could I have done better?
▷ I look at my day to be sure I practiced love and tolerance of others as my code.
▷ I reviewed my day to see that I have ceased fighting anything or anyone.

I then ask God for what corrective measures should be taken.

Date: _____   **We review our day with the God of our understanding**

Thy will be done, not mine. If we make my will the same as Your will, I will have Serenity & Peace today. Direct my thinking to be divorced from:

▷   Self Pity   ▷   Dishonesty   ▷   Self Seeking Motives   ▷   Unfounded Fears

I ask God that my thoughts do not drift into worry, remorse or morbid reflection.

May all my thoughts and actions today be sensitive & tactful without being servile or scraping.

Into Action   -   Fear of the unknown subsides when action is taken.

In thinking about my day ahead, I may be faced with indecision. I may not be able to determine which course to take.   Here I do not struggle alone. I ask God for:

       ▷   An inspiration

       ▷   An intuitive thought or decision, perhaps from his still quiet voice within

       ▷   I relax and take it easy, not forcing my will

**I look to the day ahead to these People, Actions, or Institutions
I will encounter that may bring up character defects:**

▷	**A**	Anger
▷	**R**	Resentment
▷	**SE**	Self-Esteem
▷	**$**	Financial Responsibility
▷	**D/A**	Dreams and Ambitions
▷	**PR**	Personal Relationships
▷	**F**	Fear/Frightened
▷	**L**	Laziness/Sloth
▷	**M**	Materialism
▷	**RT**	Retail Therapy
▷	**S/S**	Selfish/Self Seeking
▷	**DH**	Dishonesty
▷	**D**	Depression/Sad
▷	**J/E**	Jealous/Envy
▷	**P/E**	Pride/Ego
▷	**Fru**	Frustration

In my Thoughts & Prayers today: _____

As I finish my morning meditation and start my day, I offer this prayer to the God of my understanding:

     Here I am. For better or worse, use me as you will. May I follow the guidance of your still small voice. That voice of reason. That voice of another person or my sponsor. Or the collective voice of a home group. Use my strengths and weaknesses in a way useful to others as well as myself. May I have the strength and the courage to follow that still small voice throughout my day. May I behave with grace, sensitivity, tact, consideration and honesty in all situations I encounter this day.

Finally: I remember when I have no clear guidance from God I must go forward quietly along the path of duty.

At the end of the day (10th Step):

I look back at my actions and thoughts during the day just passed, and ask:

     ▷   Was I resentful, selfish, dishonest, or afraid in my words and/or actions?

     ▷   Do I owe anyone an apology?

     ▷   Have I kept something to myself which should have been discussed with another person at once?

     ▷   Was I kind and loving toward all?

     ▷   What could I have done better?

     ▷   I look at my day to be sure I practiced love and tolerance of others as my code.

     ▷   I reviewed my day to see that I have ceased fighting anything or anyone.

I then ask God for what corrective measures should be taken.

The day ahead... the day just passed.   Date:

Thy will be done, not mine. If we make my will the same as Your will, I will have Serenity & Peace today. Direct my thinking to be divorced from:

▷ Self Pity   ▷ Dishonesty   ▷ Self Seeking Motives   ▷ Unfounded Fears

I ask God that my thoughts do not drift into worry, remorse or morbid reflection.
May all my thoughts and actions today be sensitive & tactful without being servile or scraping.

Into Action   -   Fear of the unknown subsides when action is taken.

In thinking about my day ahead, I may be faced with indecision. I may not be able to determine which course to take.   Here I do not struggle alone. I ask God for:

> ▷ An inspiration
> ▷ An intuitive thought or decision, perhaps from his still quiet voice within
> ▷ I relax and take it easy, not forcing my will

I look to the day ahead to these People, Actions, or Institutions
I will encounter that may bring up character defects:

▷	**A**	Anger
▷	**R**	Resentment
▷	**SE**	Self-Esteem
▷	**$**	Financial Responsibility
▷	**D/A**	Dreams and Ambitions
▷	**PR**	Personal Relationships
▷	**F**	Fear/Frightened
▷	**L**	Laziness/Sloth
▷	**M**	Materialism
▷	**RT**	Retail Therapy
▷	**S/S**	Selfish/Self Seeking
▷	**DH**	Dishonesty
▷	**D**	Depression/Sad
▷	**J/E**	Jealous/Envy
▷	**P/E**	Pride/Ego
▷	**Fru**	Frustration

In my Thoughts & Prayers today:

As I finish my morning meditation and start my day, I offer this prayer to the God of my understanding:
Here I am. For better or worse, use me as you will. May I follow the guidance of your still small voice. That voice of reason. That voice of another person or my sponsor. Or the collective voice of a home group. Use my strengths and weaknesses in a way useful to others as well as myself. May I have the strength and the courage to follow that still small voice throughout my day. May I behave with grace, sensitivity, tact, consideration and honesty in all situations I encounter this day.

Finally: I remember when I have no clear guidance from God I must go forward quietly along the path of duty.

At the end of the day (10th Step):

I look back at my actions and thoughts during the day just passed, and ask:

> ▷ Was I resentful, selfish, dishonest, or afraid in my words and/or actions?
> ▷ Do I owe anyone an apology?
> ▷ Have I kept something to myself which should have been discussed with another person at once?
> ▷ Was I kind and loving toward all?
> ▷ What could I have done better?
> ▷ I look at my day to be sure I practiced love and tolerance of others as my code.
> ▷ I reviewed my day to see that I have ceased fighting anything or anyone.

I then ask God for what corrective measures should be taken.

Date: _____ **We review our day with the God of our understanding**

Thy will be done, not mine. If we make my will the same as Your will, I will have Serenity & Peace today.
Direct my thinking to be divorced from:
  ▷ Self Pity   ▷ Dishonesty   ▷ Self Seeking Motives   ▷ Unfounded Fears
I ask God that my thoughts do not drift into worry, remorse or morbid reflection.
May all my thoughts and actions today be sensitive & tactful without being servile or scraping.

Into Action   -   Fear of the unknown subsides when action is taken.

In thinking about my day ahead, I may be faced with indecision. I may not be able to determine which course to take.   Here I do not struggle alone. I ask God for:
  ▷ An inspiration
  ▷ An intuitive thought or decision, perhaps from his still quiet voice within
  ▷ I relax and take it easy, not forcing my will

I look to the day ahead to these People, Actions, or Institutions
I will encounter that may bring up character defects:

▷	**A**	Anger
▷	**R**	Resentment
▷	**SE**	Self-Esteem
▷	**$**	Financial Responsibility
▷	**D/A**	Dreams and Ambitions
▷	**PR**	Personal Relationships
▷	**F**	Fear/Frightened
▷	**L**	Laziness/Sloth
▷	**M**	Materialism
▷	**RT**	Retail Therapy
▷	**S/S**	Selfish/Self Seeking
▷	**DH**	Dishonesty
▷	**D**	Depression/Sad
▷	**J/E**	Jealous/Envy
▷	**P/E**	Pride/Ego
▷	**Fru**	Frustration

In my Thoughts & Prayers today: _____

As I finish my morning meditation and start my day, I offer this prayer to the God of my understanding:
    Here I am. For better or worse, use me as you will. May I follow the guidance of your still small voice. That voice of reason. That voice of another person or my sponsor. Or the collective voice of a home group. Use my strengths and weaknesses in a way useful to others as well as myself. May I have the strength and the courage to follow that still small voice throughout my day. May I behave with grace, sensitivity, tact, consideration and honesty in all situations I encounter this day.

Finally: I remember when I have no clear guidance from God I must go forward quietly along the path of duty.

At the end of the day (10th Step):
I look back at my actions and thoughts during the day just passed, and ask:
  ▷ Was I resentful, selfish, dishonest, or afraid in my words and/or actions?
  ▷ Do I owe anyone an apology?
  ▷ Have I kept something to myself which should have been discussed with another person at once?
  ▷ Was I kind and loving toward all?
  ▷ What could I have done better?
  ▷ I look at my day to be sure I practiced love and tolerance of others as my code.
  ▷ I reviewed my day to see that I have ceased fighting anything or anyone.
I then ask God for what corrective measures should be taken.

The day ahead... the day just passed.   Date:

Date: _____   **We review our day with the God of our understanding**
_____

Thy will be done, not mine. If we make my will the same as Your will, I will have Serenity & Peace today.
Direct my thinking to be divorced from:

  ▷ Self Pity   ▷ Dishonesty   ▷ Self Seeking Motives   ▷ Unfounded Fears

I ask God that my thoughts do not drift into worry, remorse or morbid reflection.
May all my thoughts and actions today be sensitive & tactful without being servile or scraping.

Into Action   -   Fear of the unknown subsides when action is taken.
_____

In thinking about my day ahead, I may be faced with indecision. I may not be able to determine which course to take.   Here I do not struggle alone. I ask God for:

  ▷ An inspiration
  ▷ An intuitive thought or decision, perhaps from his still quiet voice within
  ▷ I relax and take it easy, not forcing my will

**I look to the day ahead to these People, Actions, or Institutions
I will encounter that may bring up character defects:**

▷	**A**	Anger
▷	**R**	Resentment
▷	**SE**	Self-Esteem
▷	**$**	Financial Responsibility
▷	**D/A**	Dreams and Ambitions
▷	**PR**	Personal Relationships
▷	**F**	Fear/Frightened
▷	**L**	Laziness/Sloth
▷	**M**	Materialism
▷	**RT**	Retail Therapy
▷	**S/S**	Selfish/Self Seeking
▷	**DH**	Dishonesty
▷	**D**	Depression/Sad
▷	**J/E**	Jealous/Envy
▷	**P/E**	Pride/Ego
▷	**Fru**	Frustration

In my Thoughts & Prayers today: _____

As I finish my morning meditation and start my day, I offer this prayer to the God of my understanding:
Here I am. For better or worse, use me as you will. May I follow the guidance of your still small voice. That voice of reason. That voice of another person or my sponsor. Or the collective voice of a home group. Use my strengths and weaknesses in a way useful to others as well as myself. May I have the strength and the courage to follow that still small voice throughout my day. May I behave with grace, sensitivity, tact, consideration and honesty in all situations I encounter this day.

Finally: I remember when I have no clear guidance from God I must go forward quietly along the path of duty.
_____

At the end of the day (10th Step):
I look back at my actions and thoughts during the day just passed, and ask:

  ▷ Was I resentful, selfish, dishonest, or afraid in my words and/or actions?
  ▷ Do I owe anyone an apology?
  ▷ Have I kept something to myself which should have been discussed with another person at once?
  ▷ Was I kind and loving toward all?
  ▷ What could I have done better?
  ▷ I look at my day to be sure I practiced love and tolerance of others as my code.
  ▷ I reviewed my day to see that I have ceased fighting anything or anyone.

I then ask God for what corrective measures should be taken.

The day ahead... the day just passed.   Date:

Date: _____ **We review our day with the God of our understanding**

Thy will be done, not mine. If we make my will the same as Your will, I will have Serenity & Peace today.
Direct my thinking to be divorced from:

▷ Self Pity   ▷ Dishonesty   ▷ Self Seeking Motives   ▷ Unfounded Fears

I ask God that my thoughts do not drift into worry, remorse or morbid reflection.
May all my thoughts and actions today be sensitive & tactful without being servile or scraping.

Into Action   -   Fear of the unknown subsides when action is taken.

In thinking about my day ahead, I may be faced with indecision. I may not be able to determine which course to take.   Here I do not struggle alone. I ask God for:

▷ An inspiration

▷ An intuitive thought or decision, perhaps from his still quiet voice within

▷ I relax and take it easy, not forcing my will

**I look to the day ahead to these People, Actions, or Institutions
I will encounter that may bring up character defects:**

▷ **A**	Anger
▷ **R**	Resentment
▷ **SE**	Self-Esteem
▷ **$**	Financial Responsibility
▷ **D/A**	Dreams and Ambitions
▷ **PR**	Personal Relationships
▷ **F**	Fear/Frightened
▷ **L**	Laziness/Sloth
▷ **M**	Materialism
▷ **RT**	Retail Therapy
▷ **S/S**	Selfish/Self Seeking
▷ **DH**	Dishonesty
▷ **D**	Depression/Sad
▷ **J/E**	Jealous/Envy
▷ **P/E**	Pride/Ego
▷ **Fru**	Frustration

In my Thoughts & Prayers today: _____

As I finish my morning meditation and start my day, I offer this prayer to the God of my understanding:
Here I am. For better or worse, use me as you will. May I follow the guidance of your still small voice. That voice of reason. That voice of another person or my sponsor. Or the collective voice of a home group. Use my strengths and weaknesses in a way useful to others as well as myself. May I have the strength and the courage to follow that still small voice throughout my day. May I behave with grace, sensitivity, tact, consideration and honesty in all situations I encounter this day.

Finally: I remember when I have no clear guidance from God I must go forward quietly along the path of duty.

At the end of the day (10th Step):
I look back at my actions and thoughts during the day just passed, and ask:

▷ Was I resentful, selfish, dishonest, or afraid in my words and/or actions?

▷ Do I owe anyone an apology?

▷ Have I kept something to myself which should have been discussed with another person at once?

▷ Was I kind and loving toward all?

▷ What could I have done better?

▷ I look at my day to be sure I practiced love and tolerance of others as my code.

▷ I reviewed my day to see that I have ceased fighting anything or anyone.

I then ask God for what corrective measures should be taken.

The day ahead... the day just passed.   Date:

Date: **We review our day with the God of our understanding**

Thy will be done, not mine. If we make my will the same as Your will, I will have Serenity & Peace today.
Direct my thinking to be divorced from:

   ▷ Self Pity   ▷ Dishonesty   ▷ Self Seeking Motives   ▷ Unfounded Fears

I ask God that my thoughts do not drift into worry, remorse or morbid reflection.
May all my thoughts and actions today be sensitive & tactful without being servile or scraping.

Into Action   -   Fear of the unknown subsides when action is taken.

In thinking about my day ahead, I may be faced with indecision. I may not be able to determine which course to take.   Here I do not struggle alone. I ask God for:

         ▷ An inspiration
         ▷ An intuitive thought or decision, perhaps from his still quiet voice within
         ▷ I relax and take it easy, not forcing my will

**I look to the day ahead to these People, Actions, or Institutions
I will encounter that may bring up character defects:**

▷	**A**	Anger
▷	**R**	Resentment
▷	**SE**	Self-Esteem
▷	**$**	Financial Responsibility
▷	**D/A**	Dreams and Ambitions
▷	**PR**	Personal Relationships
▷	**F**	Fear/Frightened
▷	**L**	Laziness/Sloth
▷	**M**	Materialism
▷	**RT**	Retail Therapy
▷	**S/S**	Selfish/Self Seeking
▷	**DH**	Dishonesty
▷	**D**	Depression/Sad
▷	**J/E**	Jealous/Envy
▷	**P/E**	Pride/Ego
▷	**Fru**	Frustration

In my Thoughts & Prayers today:

As I finish my morning meditation and start my day, I offer this prayer to the God of my understanding:
Here I am. For better or worse, use me as you will. May I follow the guidance of your still small voice. That voice of reason. That voice of another person or my sponsor. Or the collective voice of a home group. Use my strengths and weaknesses in a way useful to others as well as myself. May I have the strength and the courage to follow that still small voice throughout my day. May I behave with grace, sensitivity, tact, consideration and honesty in all situations I encounter this day.

Finally: I remember when I have no clear guidance from God I must go forward quietly along the path of duty.

At the end of the day (10th Step):
I look back at my actions and thoughts during the day just passed, and ask:

     ▷ Was I resentful, selfish, dishonest, or afraid in my words and/or actions?
     ▷ Do I owe anyone an apology?
     ▷ Have I kept something to myself which should have been discussed with another person at once?
     ▷ Was I kind and loving toward all?
     ▷ What could I have done better?
     ▷ I look at my day to be sure I practiced love and tolerance of others as my code.
     ▷ I reviewed my day to see that I have ceased fighting anything or anyone.

I then ask God for what corrective measures should be taken.

Date: _____ **We review our day with the God of our understanding**

Thy will be done, not mine. If we make my will the same as Your will, I will have Serenity & Peace today.
Direct my thinking to be divorced from:

▷ Self Pity ▷ Dishonesty ▷ Self Seeking Motives ▷ Unfounded Fears

I ask God that my thoughts do not drift into worry, remorse or morbid reflection.
May all my thoughts and actions today be sensitive & tactful without being servile or scraping.

Into Action - Fear of the unknown subsides when action is taken.

In thinking about my day ahead, I may be faced with indecision. I may not be able to determine which course to take. Here I do not struggle alone. I ask God for:

▷ An inspiration
▷ An intuitive thought or decision, perhaps from his still quiet voice within
▷ I relax and take it easy, not forcing my will

I look to the day ahead to these People, Actions, or Institutions
I will encounter that may bring up character defects:

▷	**A**	Anger
▷	**R**	Resentment
▷	**SE**	Self-Esteem
▷	**$**	Financial Responsibility
▷	**D/A**	Dreams and Ambitions
▷	**PR**	Personal Relationships
▷	**F**	Fear/Frightened
▷	**L**	Laziness/Sloth
▷	**M**	Materialism
▷	**RT**	Retail Therapy
▷	**S/S**	Selfish/Self Seeking
▷	**DH**	Dishonesty
▷	**D**	Depression/Sad
▷	**J/E**	Jealous/Envy
▷	**P/E**	Pride/Ego
▷	**Fru**	Frustration

In my Thoughts & Prayers today: _____

As I finish my morning meditation and start my day, I offer this prayer to the God of my understanding:

Here I am. For better or worse, use me as you will. May I follow the guidance of your still small voice. That voice of reason. That voice of another person or my sponsor. Or the collective voice of a home group. Use my strengths and weaknesses in a way useful to others as well as myself. May I have the strength and the courage to follow that still small voice throughout my day. May I behave with grace, sensitivity, tact, consideration and honesty in all situations I encounter this day.

Finally: I remember when I have no clear guidance from God I must go forward quietly along the path of duty.

At the end of the day (10th Step):

I look back at my actions and thoughts during the day just passed, and ask:

▷ Was I resentful, selfish, dishonest, or afraid in my words and/or actions?
▷ Do I owe anyone an apology?
▷ Have I kept something to myself which should have been discussed with another person at once?
▷ Was I kind and loving toward all?
▷ What could I have done better?
▷ I look at my day to be sure I practiced love and tolerance of others as my code.
▷ I reviewed my day to see that I have ceased fighting anything or anyone.

I then ask God for what corrective measures should be taken.

The day ahead... the day just passed.   Date:

Date: _____ **We review our day with the God of our understanding**

Thy will be done, not mine. If we make my will the same as Your will, I will have Serenity & Peace today. Direct my thinking to be divorced from:

 ▷ Self Pity ▷ Dishonesty ▷ Self Seeking Motives ▷ Unfounded Fears

I ask God that my thoughts do not drift into worry, remorse or morbid reflection.

May all my thoughts and actions today be sensitive & tactful without being servile or scraping.

Into Action - Fear of the unknown subsides when action is taken.

In thinking about my day ahead, I may be faced with indecision. I may not be able to determine which course to take. Here I do not struggle alone. I ask God for:

 ▷ An inspiration
 ▷ An intuitive thought or decision, perhaps from his still quiet voice within
 ▷ I relax and take it easy, not forcing my will

I look to the day ahead to these People, Actions, or Institutions I will encounter that may bring up character defects:

_____

_____

_____

_____

_____

_____

_____

_____

_____

_____

_____

▷	**A**	Anger
▷	**R**	Resentment
▷	**SE**	Self-Esteem
▷	**$**	Financial Responsibility
▷	**D/A**	Dreams and Ambitions
▷	**PR**	Personal Relationships
▷	**F**	Fear/Frightened
▷	**L**	Laziness/Sloth
▷	**M**	Materialism
▷	**RT**	Retail Therapy
▷	**S/S**	Selfish/Self Seeking
▷	**DH**	Dishonesty
▷	**D**	Depression/Sad
▷	**J/E**	Jealous/Envy
▷	**P/E**	Pride/Ego
▷	**Fru**	Frustration

In my Thoughts & Prayers today: _____

As I finish my morning meditation and start my day, I offer this prayer to the God of my understanding:

Here I am. For better or worse, use me as you will. May I follow the guidance of your still small voice. That voice of reason. That voice of another person or my sponsor. Or the collective voice of a home group. Use my strengths and weaknesses in a way useful to others as well as myself. May I have the strength and the courage to follow that still small voice throughout my day. May I behave with grace, sensitivity, tact, consideration and honesty in all situations I encounter this day.

Finally: I remember when I have no clear guidance from God I must go forward quietly along the path of duty.

At the end of the day (10th Step):

I look back at my actions and thoughts during the day just passed, and ask:

 ▷ Was I resentful, selfish, dishonest, or afraid in my words and/or actions?
 ▷ Do I owe anyone an apology?
 ▷ Have I kept something to myself which should have been discussed with another person at once?
 ▷ Was I kind and loving toward all?
 ▷ What could I have done better?
 ▷ I look at my day to be sure I practiced love and tolerance of others as my code.
 ▷ I reviewed my day to see that I have ceased fighting anything or anyone.

I then ask God for what corrective measures should be taken.

Date: _____ **We review our day with the God of our understanding**

Thy will be done, not mine. If we make my will the same as Your will, I will have Serenity & Peace today.
Direct my thinking to be divorced from:

   ▷ Self Pity   ▷ Dishonesty   ▷ Self Seeking Motives   ▷ Unfounded Fears

I ask God that my thoughts do not drift into worry, remorse or morbid reflection.
May all my thoughts and actions today be sensitive & tactful without being servile or scraping.

Into Action   -   Fear of the unknown subsides when action is taken.

In thinking about my day ahead, I may be faced with indecision. I may not be able to determine which course to take.   Here I do not struggle alone. I ask God for:

      ▷ An inspiration
      ▷ An intuitive thought or decision, perhaps from his still quiet voice within
      ▷ I relax and take it easy, not forcing my will

**I look to the day ahead to these People, Actions, or Institutions
I will encounter that may bring up character defects:**

▷	**A**	Anger
▷	**R**	Resentment
▷	**SE**	Self-Esteem
▷	**$**	Financial Responsibility
▷	**D/A**	Dreams and Ambitions
▷	**PR**	Personal Relationships
▷	**F**	Fear/Frightened
▷	**L**	Laziness/Sloth
▷	**M**	Materialism
▷	**RT**	Retail Therapy
▷	**S/S**	Selfish/Self Seeking
▷	**DH**	Dishonesty
▷	**D**	Depression/Sad
▷	**J/E**	Jealous/Envy
▷	**P/E**	Pride/Ego
▷	**Fru**	Frustration

In my Thoughts & Prayers today: _____

As I finish my morning meditation and start my day, I offer this prayer to the God of my understanding:

    Here I am. For better or worse, use me as you will. May I follow the guidance of your still small voice. That voice of reason. That voice of another person or my sponsor. Or the collective voice of a home group. Use my strengths and weaknesses in a way useful to others as well as myself. May I have the strength and the courage to follow that still small voice throughout my day. May I behave with grace, sensitivity, tact, consideration and honesty in all situations I encounter this day.

Finally: I remember when I have no clear guidance from God I must go forward quietly along the path of duty.

At the end of the day (10th Step):

I look back at my actions and thoughts during the day just passed, and ask:

    ▷ Was I resentful, selfish, dishonest, or afraid in my words and/or actions?
    ▷ Do I owe anyone an apology?
    ▷ Have I kept something to myself which should have been discussed with another person at once?
    ▷ Was I kind and loving toward all?
    ▷ What could I have done better?
    ▷ I look at my day to be sure I practiced love and tolerance of others as my code.
    ▷ I reviewed my day to see that I have ceased fighting anything or anyone.

I then ask God for what corrective measures should be taken.

The day ahead... the day just passed.   Date:

Date: _____ **We review our day with the God of our understanding**

Thy will be done, not mine. If we make my will the same as Your will, I will have Serenity & Peace today.
Direct my thinking to be divorced from:

> Self Pity   > Dishonesty   > Self Seeking Motives   > Unfounded Fears

I ask God that my thoughts do not drift into worry, remorse or morbid reflection.
May all my thoughts and actions today be sensitive & tactful without being servile or scraping.

Into Action   -   Fear of the unknown subsides when action is taken.

In thinking about my day ahead, I may be faced with indecision. I may not be able to determine which course to take. Here I do not struggle alone. I ask God for:

> An inspiration
> An intuitive thought or decision, perhaps from his still quiet voice within
> I relax and take it easy, not forcing my will

**I look to the day ahead to these People, Actions, or Institutions
I will encounter that may bring up character defects:**

>	**A**	Anger
>	**R**	Resentment
>	**SE**	Self-Esteem
>	**$**	Financial Responsibility
>	**D/A**	Dreams and Ambitions
>	**PR**	Personal Relationships
>	**F**	Fear/Frightened
>	**L**	Laziness/Sloth
>	**M**	Materialism
>	**RT**	Retail Therapy
>	**S/S**	Selfish/Self Seeking
>	**DH**	Dishonesty
>	**D**	Depression/Sad
>	**J/E**	Jealous/Envy
>	**P/E**	Pride/Ego
>	**Fru**	Frustration

In my Thoughts & Prayers today: _____

As I finish my morning meditation and start my day, I offer this prayer to the God of my understanding:
Here I am. For better or worse, use me as you will. May I follow the guidance of your still small voice. That voice of reason. That voice of another person or my sponsor. Or the collective voice of a home group. Use my strengths and weaknesses in a way useful to others as well as myself. May I have the strength and the courage to follow that still small voice throughout my day. May I behave with grace, sensitivity, tact, consideration and honesty in all situations I encounter this day.

Finally: I remember when I have no clear guidance from God I must go forward quietly along the path of duty.

At the end of the day (10th Step):
I look back at my actions and thoughts during the day just passed, and ask:

> Was I resentful, selfish, dishonest, or afraid in my words and/or actions?
> Do I owe anyone an apology?
> Have I kept something to myself which should have been discussed with another person at once?
> Was I kind and loving toward all?
> What could I have done better?
> I look at my day to be sure I practiced love and tolerance of others as my code.
> I reviewed my day to see that I have ceased fighting anything or anyone.

I then ask God for what corrective measures should be taken.

Date: _____ **We review our day with the God of our understanding**

Thy will be done, not mine. If we make my will the same as Your will, I will have Serenity & Peace today. Direct my thinking to be divorced from:

▷ Self Pity   ▷ Dishonesty   ▷ Self Seeking Motives   ▷ Unfounded Fears

I ask God that my thoughts do not drift into worry, remorse or morbid reflection.
May all my thoughts and actions today be sensitive & tactful without being servile or scraping.

Into Action   -   Fear of the unknown subsides when action is taken.

In thinking about my day ahead, I may be faced with indecision. I may not be able to determine which course to take.   Here I do not struggle alone. I ask God for:

▷ An inspiration
▷ An intuitive thought or decision, perhaps from his still quiet voice within
▷ I relax and take it easy, not forcing my will

**I look to the day ahead to these People, Actions, or Institutions
I will encounter that may bring up character defects:**

▷	**A**	Anger
▷	**R**	Resentment
▷	**SE**	Self-Esteem
▷	**$**	Financial Responsibility
▷	**D/A**	Dreams and Ambitions
▷	**PR**	Personal Relationships
▷	**F**	Fear/Frightened
▷	**L**	Laziness/Sloth
▷	**M**	Materialism
▷	**RT**	Retail Therapy
▷	**S/S**	Selfish/Self Seeking
▷	**DH**	Dishonesty
▷	**D**	Depression/Sad
▷	**J/E**	Jealous/Envy
▷	**P/E**	Pride/Ego
▷	**Fru**	Frustration

In my Thoughts & Prayers today: _____

As I finish my morning meditation and start my day, I offer this prayer to the God of my understanding:

Here I am. For better or worse, use me as you will. May I follow the guidance of your still small voice. That voice of reason. That voice of another person or my sponsor. Or the collective voice of a home group. Use my strengths and weaknesses in a way useful to others as well as myself. May I have the strength and the courage to follow that still small voice throughout my day. May I behave with grace, sensitivity, tact, consideration and honesty in all situations I encounter this day.

Finally: I remember when I have no clear guidance from God I must go forward quietly along the path of duty.

At the end of the day (10th Step):

I look back at my actions and thoughts during the day just passed, and ask:

▷   Was I resentful, selfish, dishonest, or afraid in my words and/or actions?
▷   Do I owe anyone an apology?
▷   Have I kept something to myself which should have been discussed with another person at once?
▷   Was I kind and loving toward all?
▷   What could I have done better?
▷   I look at my day to be sure I practiced love and tolerance of others as my code.
▷   I reviewed my day to see that I have ceased fighting anything or anyone.

I then ask God for what corrective measures should be taken.

The day ahead... the day just passed.   Date:

Date: _____ **We review our day with the God of our understanding**

Thy will be done, not mine. If we make my will the same as Your will, I will have Serenity & Peace today.
Direct my thinking to be divorced from:

▷ Self Pity   ▷ Dishonesty   ▷ Self Seeking Motives   ▷ Unfounded Fears

I ask God that my thoughts do not drift into worry, remorse or morbid reflection.
May all my thoughts and actions today be sensitive & tactful without being servile or scraping.

Into Action   -   Fear of the unknown subsides when action is taken.

In thinking about my day ahead, I may be faced with indecision. I may not be able to determine which course to take.   Here I do not struggle alone. I ask God for:

  ▷ An inspiration
  ▷ An intuitive thought or decision, perhaps from his still quiet voice within
  ▷ I relax and take it easy, not forcing my will

**I look to the day ahead to these People, Actions, or Institutions
I will encounter that may bring up character defects:**

▷	**A**	Anger
▷	**R**	Resentment
▷	**SE**	Self-Esteem
▷	**$**	Financial Responsibility
▷	**D/A**	Dreams and Ambitions
▷	**PR**	Personal Relationships
▷	**F**	Fear/Frightened
▷	**L**	Laziness/Sloth
▷	**M**	Materialism
▷	**RT**	Retail Therapy
▷	**S/S**	Selfish/Self Seeking
▷	**DH**	Dishonesty
▷	**D**	Depression/Sad
▷	**J/E**	Jealous/Envy
▷	**P/E**	Pride/Ego
▷	**Fru**	Frustration

In my Thoughts & Prayers today: _____

As I finish my morning meditation and start my day, I offer this prayer to the God of my understanding:
Here I am. For better or worse, use me as you will. May I follow the guidance of your still small voice. That voice of reason. That voice of another person or my sponsor. Or the collective voice of a home group. Use my strengths and weaknesses in a way useful to others as well as myself. May I have the strength and the courage to follow that still small voice throughout my day. May I behave with grace, sensitivity, tact, consideration and honesty in all situations I encounter this day.

Finally: I remember when I have no clear guidance from God I must go forward quietly along the path of duty.

At the end of the day (10th Step):

I look back at my actions and thoughts during the day just passed, and ask:

  ▷ Was I resentful, selfish, dishonest, or afraid in my words and/or actions?
  ▷ Do I owe anyone an apology?
  ▷ Have I kept something to myself which should have been discussed with another person at once?
  ▷ Was I kind and loving toward all?
  ▷ What could I have done better?
  ▷ I look at my day to be sure I practiced love and tolerance of others as my code.
  ▷ I reviewed my day to see that I have ceased fighting anything or anyone.

I then ask God for what corrective measures should be taken.

Date: _____   **We review our day with the God of our understanding**

Thy will be done, not mine. If we make my will the same as Your will, I will have Serenity & Peace today.
Direct my thinking to be divorced from:

  ▷   Self Pity   ▷   Dishonesty   ▷   Self Seeking Motives   ▷   Unfounded Fears

I ask God that my thoughts do not drift into worry, remorse or morbid reflection.
May all my thoughts and actions today be sensitive & tactful without being servile or scraping.

Into Action   -   Fear of the unknown subsides when action is taken.

In thinking about my day ahead, I may be faced with indecision. I may not be able to determine which course to take.   Here I do not struggle alone. I ask God for:

         ▷   An inspiration
         ▷   An intuitive thought or decision, perhaps from his still quiet voice within
         ▷   I relax and take it easy, not forcing my will

**I look to the day ahead to these People, Actions, or Institutions
I will encounter that may bring up character defects:**

▷	**A**	Anger
▷	**R**	Resentment
▷	**SE**	Self-Esteem
▷	**$**	Financial Responsibility
▷	**D/A**	Dreams and Ambitions
▷	**PR**	Personal Relationships
▷	**F**	Fear/Frightened
▷	**L**	Laziness/Sloth
▷	**M**	Materialism
▷	**RT**	Retail Therapy
▷	**S/S**	Selfish/Self Seeking
▷	**DH**	Dishonesty
▷	**D**	Depression/Sad
▷	**J/E**	Jealous/Envy
▷	**P/E**	Pride/Ego
▷	**Fru**	Frustration

In my Thoughts & Prayers today: _____

As I finish my morning meditation and start my day, I offer this prayer to the God of my understanding:

Here I am. For better or worse, use me as you will. May I follow the guidance of your still small voice. That voice of reason. That voice of another person or my sponsor. Or the collective voice of a home group. Use my strengths and weaknesses in a way useful to others as well as myself. May I have the strength and the courage to follow that still small voice throughout my day. May I behave with grace, sensitivity, tact, consideration and honesty in all situations I encounter this day.

Finally: I remember when I have no clear guidance from God I must go forward quietly along the path of duty.

At the end of the day (10th Step):

I look back at my actions and thoughts during the day just passed, and ask:

       ▷   Was I resentful, selfish, dishonest, or afraid in my words and/or actions?
       ▷   Do I owe anyone an apology?
       ▷   Have I kept something to myself which should have been discussed with another person at once?
       ▷   Was I kind and loving toward all?
       ▷   What could I have done better?
       ▷   I look at my day to be sure I practiced love and tolerance of others as my code.
       ▷   I reviewed my day to see that I have ceased fighting anything or anyone.

I then ask God for what corrective measures should be taken.

Date: _____ **We review our day with the God of our understanding**

Thy will be done, not mine. If we make my will the same as Your will, I will have Serenity & Peace today.
Direct my thinking to be divorced from:

▷ Self Pity ▷ Dishonesty ▷ Self Seeking Motives ▷ Unfounded Fears

I ask God that my thoughts do not drift into worry, remorse or morbid reflection.
May all my thoughts and actions today be sensitive & tactful without being servile or scraping.

Into Action - Fear of the unknown subsides when action is taken.

In thinking about my day ahead, I may be faced with indecision. I may not be able to determine which course to take. Here I do not struggle alone. I ask God for:

▷ An inspiration
▷ An intuitive thought or decision, perhaps from his still quiet voice within
▷ I relax and take it easy, not forcing my will

**I look to the day ahead to these People, Actions, or Institutions
I will encounter that may bring up character defects:**

▷	**A**	Anger
▷	**R**	Resentment
▷	**SE**	Self-Esteem
▷	**$**	Financial Responsibility
▷	**D/A**	Dreams and Ambitions
▷	**PR**	Personal Relationships
▷	**F**	Fear/Frightened
▷	**L**	Laziness/Sloth
▷	**M**	Materialism
▷	**RT**	Retail Therapy
▷	**S/S**	Selfish/Self Seeking
▷	**DH**	Dishonesty
▷	**D**	Depression/Sad
▷	**J/E**	Jealous/Envy
▷	**P/E**	Pride/Ego
▷	**Fru**	Frustration

In my Thoughts & Prayers today: _____

As I finish my morning meditation and start my day, I offer this prayer to the God of my understanding:

Here I am. For better or worse, use me as you will. May I follow the guidance of your still small voice. That voice of reason. That voice of another person or my sponsor. Or the collective voice of a home group. Use my strengths and weaknesses in a way useful to others as well as myself. May I have the strength and the courage to follow that still small voice throughout my day. May I behave with grace, sensitivity, tact, consideration and honesty in all situations I encounter this day.

Finally: I remember when I have no clear guidance from God I must go forward quietly along the path of duty.

At the end of the day (10th Step):

I look back at my actions and thoughts during the day just passed, and ask:

▷ Was I resentful, selfish, dishonest, or afraid in my words and/or actions?
▷ Do I owe anyone an apology?
▷ Have I kept something to myself which should have been discussed with another person at once?
▷ Was I kind and loving toward all?
▷ What could I have done better?
▷ I look at my day to be sure I practiced love and tolerance of others as my code.
▷ I reviewed my day to see that I have ceased fighting anything or anyone.

I then ask God for what corrective measures should be taken.

The day ahead... the day just passed.   Date:

Date: _____ **We review our day with the God of our understanding**

Thy will be done, not mine. If we make my will the same as Your will, I will have Serenity & Peace today.
Direct my thinking to be divorced from:

  ▷ Self Pity ▷ Dishonesty ▷ Self Seeking Motives ▷ Unfounded Fears

I ask God that my thoughts do not drift into worry, remorse or morbid reflection.
May all my thoughts and actions today be sensitive & tactful without being servile or scraping.

Into Action - Fear of the unknown subsides when action is taken.

In thinking about my day ahead, I may be faced with indecision. I may not be able to determine which course to take. Here I do not struggle alone. I ask God for:

  ▷ An inspiration
  ▷ An intuitive thought or decision, perhaps from his still quiet voice within
  ▷ I relax and take it easy, not forcing my will

I look to the day ahead to these People, Actions, or Institutions
I will encounter that may bring up character defects:

▷	**A**	Anger
▷	**R**	Resentment
▷	**SE**	Self-Esteem
▷	**$**	Financial Responsibility
▷	**D/A**	Dreams and Ambitions
▷	**PR**	Personal Relationships
▷	**F**	Fear/Frightened
▷	**L**	Laziness/Sloth
▷	**M**	Materialism
▷	**RT**	Retail Therapy
▷	**S/S**	Selfish/Self Seeking
▷	**DH**	Dishonesty
▷	**D**	Depression/Sad
▷	**J/E**	Jealous/Envy
▷	**P/E**	Pride/Ego
▷	**Fru**	Frustration

In my Thoughts & Prayers today: _____

As I finish my morning meditation and start my day, I offer this prayer to the God of my understanding:
Here I am. For better or worse, use me as you will. May I follow the guidance of your still small voice. That voice of reason. That voice of another person or my sponsor. Or the collective voice of a home group. Use my strengths and weaknesses in a way useful to others as well as myself. May I have the strength and the courage to follow that still small voice throughout my day. May I behave with grace, sensitivity, tact, consideration and honesty in all situations I encounter this day.

Finally: I remember when I have no clear guidance from God I must go forward quietly along the path of duty.

At the end of the day (10th Step):

I look back at my actions and thoughts during the day just passed, and ask:

  ▷ Was I resentful, selfish, dishonest, or afraid in my words and/or actions?
  ▷ Do I owe anyone an apology?
  ▷ Have I kept something to myself which should have been discussed with another person at once?
  ▷ Was I kind and loving toward all?
  ▷ What could I have done better?
  ▷ I look at my day to be sure I practiced love and tolerance of others as my code.
  ▷ I reviewed my day to see that I have ceased fighting anything or anyone.

I then ask God for what corrective measures should be taken.

The day ahead... the day just passed.   Date:

Date: _____ **We review our day with the God of our understanding**

Thy will be done, not mine. If we make my will the same as Your will, I will have Serenity & Peace today.
Direct my thinking to be divorced from:

▷ Self Pity   ▷ Dishonesty   ▷ Self Seeking Motives   ▷ Unfounded Fears

I ask God that my thoughts do not drift into worry, remorse or morbid reflection.
May all my thoughts and actions today be sensitive & tactful without being servile or scraping.

Into Action   -   Fear of the unknown subsides when action is taken.

In thinking about my day ahead, I may be faced with indecision. I may not be able to determine which course to take.   Here I do not struggle alone. I ask God for:

> ▷ An inspiration
> ▷ An intuitive thought or decision, perhaps from his still quiet voice within
> ▷ I relax and take it easy, not forcing my will

**I look to the day ahead to these People, Actions, or Institutions
I will encounter that may bring up character defects:**

▷	**A**	Anger
▷	**R**	Resentment
▷	**SE**	Self-Esteem
▷	**$**	Financial Responsibility
▷	**D/A**	Dreams and Ambitions
▷	**PR**	Personal Relationships
▷	**F**	Fear/Frightened
▷	**L**	Laziness/Sloth
▷	**M**	Materialism
▷	**RT**	Retail Therapy
▷	**S/S**	Selfish/Self Seeking
▷	**DH**	Dishonesty
▷	**D**	Depression/Sad
▷	**J/E**	Jealous/Envy
▷	**P/E**	Pride/Ego
▷	**Fru**	Frustration

In my Thoughts & Prayers today: _____

As I finish my morning meditation and start my day, I offer this prayer to the God of my understanding:

> Here I am. For better or worse, use me as you will. May I follow the guidance of your still small voice. That voice of reason. That voice of another person or my sponsor. Or the collective voice of a home group. Use my strengths and weaknesses in a way useful to others as well as myself. May I have the strength and the courage to follow that still small voice throughout my day. May I behave with grace, sensitivity, tact, consideration and honesty in all situations I encounter this day.

Finally: I remember when I have no clear guidance from God I must go forward quietly along the path of duty.

At the end of the day (10th Step):
I look back at my actions and thoughts during the day just passed, and ask:

> ▷ Was I resentful, selfish, dishonest, or afraid in my words and/or actions?
> ▷ Do I owe anyone an apology?
> ▷ Have I kept something to myself which should have been discussed with another person at once?
> ▷ Was I kind and loving toward all?
> ▷ What could I have done better?
> ▷ I look at my day to be sure I practiced love and tolerance of others as my code.
> ▷ I reviewed my day to see that I have ceased fighting anything or anyone.

I then ask God for what corrective measures should be taken.

Date: _____ **We review our day with the God of our understanding**

Thy will be done, not mine. If we make my will the same as Your will, I will have Serenity & Peace today.
Direct my thinking to be divorced from:
- ▷ Self Pity   ▷ Dishonesty   ▷ Self Seeking Motives   ▷ Unfounded Fears

I ask God that my thoughts do not drift into worry, remorse or morbid reflection.
May all my thoughts and actions today be sensitive & tactful without being servile or scraping.

Into Action   -   Fear of the unknown subsides when action is taken.

In thinking about my day ahead, I may be faced with indecision. I may not be able to determine which course to take. Here I do not struggle alone. I ask God for:
- ▷ An inspiration
- ▷ An intuitive thought or decision, perhaps from his still quiet voice within
- ▷ I relax and take it easy, not forcing my will

**I look to the day ahead to these People, Actions, or Institutions
I will encounter that may bring up character defects:**

▷	**A**	Anger
▷	**R**	Resentment
▷	**SE**	Self-Esteem
▷	**$**	Financial Responsibility
▷	**D/A**	Dreams and Ambitions
▷	**PR**	Personal Relationships
▷	**F**	Fear/Frightened
▷	**L**	Laziness/Sloth
▷	**M**	Materialism
▷	**RT**	Retail Therapy
▷	**S/S**	Selfish/Self Seeking
▷	**DH**	Dishonesty
▷	**D**	Depression/Sad
▷	**J/E**	Jealous/Envy
▷	**P/E**	Pride/Ego
▷	**Fru**	Frustration

In my Thoughts & Prayers today: _____

As I finish my morning meditation and start my day, I offer this prayer to the God of my understanding:
> Here I am. For better or worse, use me as you will. May I follow the guidance of your still small voice. That voice of reason. That voice of another person or my sponsor. Or the collective voice of a home group. Use my strengths and weaknesses in a way useful to others as well as myself. May I have the strength and the courage to follow that still small voice throughout my day. May I behave with grace, sensitivity, tact, consideration and honesty in all situations I encounter this day.

Finally: I remember when I have no clear guidance from God I must go forward quietly along the path of duty.

At the end of the day (10th Step):
I look back at my actions and thoughts during the day just passed, and ask:
- ▷ Was I resentful, selfish, dishonest, or afraid in my words and/or actions?
- ▷ Do I owe anyone an apology?
- ▷ Have I kept something to myself which should have been discussed with another person at once?
- ▷ Was I kind and loving toward all?
- ▷ What could I have done better?
- ▷ I look at my day to be sure I practiced love and tolerance of others as my code.
- ▷ I reviewed my day to see that I have ceased fighting anything or anyone.

I then ask God for what corrective measures should be taken.

The day ahead... the day just passed.   Date:

Date: _____ **We review our day with the God of our understanding**

Thy will be done, not mine. If we make my will the same as Your will, I will have Serenity & Peace today. Direct my thinking to be divorced from:

▷ Self Pity ▷ Dishonesty ▷ Self Seeking Motives ▷ Unfounded Fears

I ask God that my thoughts do not drift into worry, remorse or morbid reflection.

May all my thoughts and actions today be sensitive & tactful without being servile or scraping.

Into Action - Fear of the unknown subsides when action is taken.

In thinking about my day ahead, I may be faced with indecision. I may not be able to determine which course to take. Here I do not struggle alone. I ask God for:

▷ An inspiration
▷ An intuitive thought or decision, perhaps from his still quiet voice within
▷ I relax and take it easy, not forcing my will

**I look to the day ahead to these People, Actions, or Institutions
I will encounter that may bring up character defects:**

_____

▷	**A**	Anger
▷	**R**	Resentment
▷	**SE**	Self-Esteem
▷	**$**	Financial Responsibility
▷	**D/A**	Dreams and Ambitions
▷	**PR**	Personal Relationships
▷	**F**	Fear/Frightened
▷	**L**	Laziness/Sloth
▷	**M**	Materialism
▷	**RT**	Retail Therapy
▷	**S/S**	Selfish/Self Seeking
▷	**DH**	Dishonesty
▷	**D**	Depression/Sad
▷	**J/E**	Jealous/Envy
▷	**P/E**	Pride/Ego
▷	**Fru**	Frustration

In my Thoughts & Prayers today: _____

As I finish my morning meditation and start my day, I offer this prayer to the God of my understanding:

Here I am. For better or worse, use me as you will. May I follow the guidance of your still small voice. That voice of reason. That voice of another person or my sponsor. Or the collective voice of a home group. Use my strengths and weaknesses in a way useful to others as well as myself. May I have the strength and the courage to follow that still small voice throughout my day. May I behave with grace, sensitivity, tact, consideration and honesty in all situations I encounter this day.

Finally: I remember when I have no clear guidance from God I must go forward quietly along the path of duty.

At the end of the day (10th Step):

I look back at my actions and thoughts during the day just passed, and ask:

▷ Was I resentful, selfish, dishonest, or afraid in my words and/or actions?
▷ Do I owe anyone an apology?
▷ Have I kept something to myself which should have been discussed with another person at once?
▷ Was I kind and loving toward all?
▷ What could I have done better?
▷ I look at my day to be sure I practiced love and tolerance of others as my code.
▷ I reviewed my day to see that I have ceased fighting anything or anyone.

I then ask God for what corrective measures should be taken.

The day ahead... the day just passed.   Date:

Date: _____ **We review our day with the God of our understanding**

Thy will be done, not mine. If we make my will the same as Your will, I will have Serenity & Peace today.
Direct my thinking to be divorced from:

▷ Self Pity ▷ Dishonesty ▷ Self Seeking Motives ▷ Unfounded Fears

I ask God that my thoughts do not drift into worry, remorse or morbid reflection.
May all my thoughts and actions today be sensitive & tactful without being servile or scraping.

Into Action - Fear of the unknown subsides when action is taken.

In thinking about my day ahead, I may be faced with indecision. I may not be able to determine which course to take. Here I do not struggle alone. I ask God for:

▷ An inspiration
▷ An intuitive thought or decision, perhaps from his still quiet voice within
▷ I relax and take it easy, not forcing my will

**I look to the day ahead to these People, Actions, or Institutions
I will encounter that may bring up character defects:**

▷	**A**	Anger
▷	**R**	Resentment
▷	**SE**	Self-Esteem
▷	**$**	Financial Responsibility
▷	**D/A**	Dreams and Ambitions
▷	**PR**	Personal Relationships
▷	**F**	Fear/Frightened
▷	**L**	Laziness/Sloth
▷	**M**	Materialism
▷	**RT**	Retail Therapy
▷	**S/S**	Selfish/Self Seeking
▷	**DH**	Dishonesty
▷	**D**	Depression/Sad
▷	**J/E**	Jealous/Envy
▷	**P/E**	Pride/Ego
▷	**Fru**	Frustration

In my Thoughts & Prayers today: _____

As I finish my morning meditation and start my day, I offer this prayer to the God of my understanding:

Here I am. For better or worse, use me as you will. May I follow the guidance of your still small voice. That voice of reason. That voice of another person or my sponsor. Or the collective voice of a home group. Use my strengths and weaknesses in a way useful to others as well as myself. May I have the strength and the courage to follow that still small voice throughout my day. May I behave with grace, sensitivity, tact, consideration and honesty in all situations I encounter this day.

Finally: I remember when I have no clear guidance from God I must go forward quietly along the path of duty.

At the end of the day (10th Step):

I look back at my actions and thoughts during the day just passed, and ask:

▷ Was I resentful, selfish, dishonest, or afraid in my words and/or actions?
▷ Do I owe anyone an apology?
▷ Have I kept something to myself which should have been discussed with another person at once?
▷ Was I kind and loving toward all?
▷ What could I have done better?
▷ I look at my day to be sure I practiced love and tolerance of others as my code.
▷ I reviewed my day to see that I have ceased fighting anything or anyone.

I then ask God for what corrective measures should be taken.

The day ahead... the day just passed.   Date:

Date: _____ **We review our day with the God of our understanding**

Thy will be done, not mine. If we make my will the same as Your will, I will have Serenity & Peace today.
Direct my thinking to be divorced from:

▷ Self Pity   ▷ Dishonesty   ▷ Self Seeking Motives   ▷ Unfounded Fears

I ask God that my thoughts do not drift into worry, remorse or morbid reflection.
May all my thoughts and actions today be sensitive & tactful without being servile or scraping.

Into Action   -   Fear of the unknown subsides when action is taken.

In thinking about my day ahead, I may be faced with indecision. I may not be able to determine which course to take.   Here I do not struggle alone. I ask God for:

▷ An inspiration
▷ An intuitive thought or decision, perhaps from his still quiet voice within
▷ I relax and take it easy, not forcing my will

**I look to the day ahead to these People, Actions, or Institutions
I will encounter that may bring up character defects:**

▷	**A**	Anger
▷	**R**	Resentment
▷	**SE**	Self-Esteem
▷	**$**	Financial Responsibility
▷	**D/A**	Dreams and Ambitions
▷	**PR**	Personal Relationships
▷	**F**	Fear/Frightened
▷	**L**	Laziness/Sloth
▷	**M**	Materialism
▷	**RT**	Retail Therapy
▷	**S/S**	Selfish/Self Seeking
▷	**DH**	Dishonesty
▷	**D**	Depression/Sad
▷	**J/E**	Jealous/Envy
▷	**P/E**	Pride/Ego
▷	**Fru**	Frustration

In my Thoughts & Prayers today: _____

As I finish my morning meditation and start my day, I offer this prayer to the God of my understanding:
Here I am. For better or worse, use me as you will. May I follow the guidance of your still small voice. That voice of reason. That voice of another person or my sponsor. Or the collective voice of a home group. Use my strengths and weaknesses in a way useful to others as well as myself. May I have the strength and the courage to follow that still small voice throughout my day. May I behave with grace, sensitivity, tact, consideration and honesty in all situations I encounter this day.

Finally: I remember when I have no clear guidance from God I must go forward quietly along the path of duty.

At the end of the day (10th Step):

I look back at my actions and thoughts during the day just passed, and ask:

▷ Was I resentful, selfish, dishonest, or afraid in my words and/or actions?
▷ Do I owe anyone an apology?
▷ Have I kept something to myself which should have been discussed with another person at once?
▷ Was I kind and loving toward all?
▷ What could I have done better?
▷ I look at my day to be sure I practiced love and tolerance of others as my code.
▷ I reviewed my day to see that I have ceased fighting anything or anyone.

I then ask God for what corrective measures should be taken.

Date: _____ **We review our day with the God of our understanding**

Thy will be done, not mine. If we make my will the same as Your will, I will have Serenity & Peace today.
Direct my thinking to be divorced from:

▷ Self Pity ▷ Dishonesty ▷ Self Seeking Motives ▷ Unfounded Fears

I ask God that my thoughts do not drift into worry, remorse or morbid reflection.
May all my thoughts and actions today be sensitive & tactful without being servile or scraping.

Into Action - Fear of the unknown subsides when action is taken.

In thinking about my day ahead, I may be faced with indecision. I may not be able to determine which course to take. Here I do not struggle alone. I ask God for:

▷ An inspiration
▷ An intuitive thought or decision, perhaps from his still quiet voice within
▷ I relax and take it easy, not forcing my will

I look to the day ahead to these People, Actions, or Institutions
I will encounter that may bring up character defects:

▷	**A**	Anger
▷	**R**	Resentment
▷	**SE**	Self-Esteem
▷	**$**	Financial Responsibility
▷	**D/A**	Dreams and Ambitions
▷	**PR**	Personal Relationships
▷	**F**	Fear/Frightened
▷	**L**	Laziness/Sloth
▷	**M**	Materialism
▷	**RT**	Retail Therapy
▷	**S/S**	Selfish/Self Seeking
▷	**DH**	Dishonesty
▷	**D**	Depression/Sad
▷	**J/E**	Jealous/Envy
▷	**P/E**	Pride/Ego
▷	**Fru**	Frustration

In my Thoughts & Prayers today: _____

As I finish my morning meditation and start my day, I offer this prayer to the God of my understanding:
Here I am. For better or worse, use me as you will. May I follow the guidance of your still small voice. That voice of reason. That voice of another person or my sponsor. Or the collective voice of a home group. Use my strengths and weaknesses in a way useful to others as well as myself. May I have the strength and the courage to follow that still small voice throughout my day. May I behave with grace, sensitivity, tact, consideration and honesty in all situations I encounter this day.

Finally: I remember when I have no clear guidance from God I must go forward quietly along the path of duty.

At the end of the day (10ᵗʰ Step):

I look back at my actions and thoughts during the day just passed, and ask:

▷ Was I resentful, selfish, dishonest, or afraid in my words and/or actions?
▷ Do I owe anyone an apology?
▷ Have I kept something to myself which should have been discussed with another person at once?
▷ Was I kind and loving toward all?
▷ What could I have done better?
▷ I look at my day to be sure I practiced love and tolerance of others as my code.
▷ I reviewed my day to see that I have ceased fighting anything or anyone.

I then ask God for what corrective measures should be taken.

The day ahead... the day just passed.   Date:

Date: _____   **We review our day with the God of our understanding**

Thy will be done, not mine. If we make my will the same as Your will, I will have Serenity & Peace today.
Direct my thinking to be divorced from:

▷   Self Pity   ▷   Dishonesty   ▷   Self Seeking Motives   ▷   Unfounded Fears

I ask God that my thoughts do not drift into worry, remorse or morbid reflection.
May all my thoughts and actions today be sensitive & tactful without being servile or scraping.

Into Action   -   Fear of the unknown subsides when action is taken.

In thinking about my day ahead, I may be faced with indecision. I may not be able to determine which course to take.   Here I do not struggle alone. I ask God for:

         ▷   An inspiration
         ▷   An intuitive thought or decision, perhaps from his still quiet voice within
         ▷   I relax and take it easy, not forcing my will

**I look to the day ahead to these People, Actions, or Institutions
I will encounter that may bring up character defects:**

▷	**A**	Anger
▷	**R**	Resentment
▷	**SE**	Self-Esteem
▷	**$**	Financial Responsibility
▷	**D/A**	Dreams and Ambitions
▷	**PR**	Personal Relationships
▷	**F**	Fear/Frightened
▷	**L**	Laziness/Sloth
▷	**M**	Materialism
▷	**RT**	Retail Therapy
▷	**S/S**	Selfish/Self Seeking
▷	**DH**	Dishonesty
▷	**D**	Depression/Sad
▷	**J/E**	Jealous/Envy
▷	**P/E**	Pride/Ego
▷	**Fru**	Frustration

In my Thoughts & Prayers today: _____

As I finish my morning meditation and start my day, I offer this prayer to the God of my understanding:
Here I am. For better or worse, use me as you will. May I follow the guidance of your still small voice. That voice of reason. That voice of another person or my sponsor. Or the collective voice of a home group. Use my strengths and weaknesses in a way useful to others as well as myself. May I have the strength and the courage to follow that still small voice throughout my day. May I behave with grace, sensitivity, tact, consideration and honesty in all situations I encounter this day.

Finally: I remember when I have no clear guidance from God I must go forward quietly along the path of duty.

At the end of the day (10th Step)**:**

I look back at my actions and thoughts during the day just passed, and ask:

         ▷   Was I resentful, selfish, dishonest, or afraid in my words and/or actions?
         ▷   Do I owe anyone an apology?
         ▷   Have I kept something to myself which should have been discussed with another person at once?
         ▷   Was I kind and loving toward all?
         ▷   What could I have done better?
         ▷   I look at my day to be sure I practiced love and tolerance of others as my code.
         ▷   I reviewed my day to see that I have ceased fighting anything or anyone.

I then ask God for what corrective measures should be taken.

The day ahead... the day just passed.   Date:

Date: _____   **We review our day with the God of our understanding**

Thy will be done, not mine. If we make my will the same as Your will, I will have Serenity & Peace today.
Direct my thinking to be divorced from:

▷ Self Pity   ▷ Dishonesty   ▷ Self Seeking Motives   ▷ Unfounded Fears

I ask God that my thoughts do not drift into worry, remorse or morbid reflection.
May all my thoughts and actions today be sensitive & tactful without being servile or scraping.

Into Action   -   Fear of the unknown subsides when action is taken.

In thinking about my day ahead, I may be faced with indecision. I may not be able to determine which course to take.   Here I do not struggle alone. I ask God for:

▷ An inspiration
▷ An intuitive thought or decision, perhaps from his still quiet voice within
▷ I relax and take it easy, not forcing my will

**I look to the day ahead to these People, Actions, or Institutions
I will encounter that may bring up character defects:**

▷	**A**	Anger
▷	**R**	Resentment
▷	**SE**	Self-Esteem
▷	**$**	Financial Responsibility
▷	**D/A**	Dreams and Ambitions
▷	**PR**	Personal Relationships
▷	**F**	Fear/Frightened
▷	**L**	Laziness/Sloth
▷	**M**	Materialism
▷	**RT**	Retail Therapy
▷	**S/S**	Selfish/Self Seeking
▷	**DH**	Dishonesty
▷	**D**	Depression/Sad
▷	**J/E**	Jealous/Envy
▷	**P/E**	Pride/Ego
▷	**Fru**	Frustration

In my Thoughts & Prayers today: _____

As I finish my morning meditation and start my day, I offer this prayer to the God of my understanding:

Here I am. For better or worse, use me as you will. May I follow the guidance of your still small voice. That voice of reason. That voice of another person or my sponsor. Or the collective voice of a home group. Use my strengths and weaknesses in a way useful to others as well as myself. May I have the strength and the courage to follow that still small voice throughout my day. May I behave with grace, sensitivity, tact, consideration and honesty in all situations I encounter this day.

Finally: I remember when I have no clear guidance from God I must go forward quietly along the path of duty.

At the end of the day (10th Step):

I look back at my actions and thoughts during the day just passed, and ask:

▷ Was I resentful, selfish, dishonest, or afraid in my words and/or actions?
▷ Do I owe anyone an apology?
▷ Have I kept something to myself which should have been discussed with another person at once?
▷ Was I kind and loving toward all?
▷ What could I have done better?
▷ I look at my day to be sure I practiced love and tolerance of others as my code.
▷ I reviewed my day to see that I have ceased fighting anything or anyone.

I then ask God for what corrective measures should be taken.

The day ahead... the day just passed.   Date:

Date: _____ **We review our day with the God of our understanding**

Thy will be done, not mine. If we make my will the same as Your will, I will have Serenity & Peace today. Direct my thinking to be divorced from:

▷ Self Pity   ▷ Dishonesty   ▷ Self Seeking Motives   ▷ Unfounded Fears

I ask God that my thoughts do not drift into worry, remorse or morbid reflection.

May all my thoughts and actions today be sensitive & tactful without being servile or scraping.

Into Action   -   Fear of the unknown subsides when action is taken.

In thinking about my day ahead, I may be faced with indecision. I may not be able to determine which course to take.   Here I do not struggle alone. I ask God for:

▷ An inspiration
▷ An intuitive thought or decision, perhaps from his still quiet voice within
▷ I relax and take it easy, not forcing my will

I look to the day ahead to these People, Actions, or Institutions
I will encounter that may bring up character defects:

▷	**A**	Anger
▷	**R**	Resentment
▷	**SE**	Self-Esteem
▷	**$**	Financial Responsibility
▷	**D/A**	Dreams and Ambitions
▷	**PR**	Personal Relationships
▷	**F**	Fear/Frightened
▷	**L**	Laziness/Sloth
▷	**M**	Materialism
▷	**RT**	Retail Therapy
▷	**S/S**	Selfish/Self Seeking
▷	**DH**	Dishonesty
▷	**D**	Depression/Sad
▷	**J/E**	Jealous/Envy
▷	**P/E**	Pride/Ego
▷	**Fru**	Frustration

In my Thoughts & Prayers today: _____

As I finish my morning meditation and start my day, I offer this prayer to the God of my understanding:

Here I am. For better or worse, use me as you will. May I follow the guidance of your still small voice. That voice of reason. That voice of another person or my sponsor. Or the collective voice of a home group. Use my strengths and weaknesses in a way useful to others as well as myself. May I have the strength and the courage to follow that still small voice throughout my day. May I behave with grace, sensitivity, tact, consideration and honesty in all situations I encounter this day.

Finally: I remember when I have no clear guidance from God I must go forward quietly along the path of duty.

At the end of the day (10th Step):

I look back at my actions and thoughts during the day just passed, and ask:

▷ Was I resentful, selfish, dishonest, or afraid in my words and/or actions?
▷ Do I owe anyone an apology?
▷ Have I kept something to myself which should have been discussed with another person at once?
▷ Was I kind and loving toward all?
▷ What could I have done better?
▷ I look at my day to be sure I practiced love and tolerance of others as my code.
▷ I reviewed my day to see that I have ceased fighting anything or anyone.

I then ask God for what corrective measures should be taken.

The day ahead... the day just passed.   Date:

Date: _____ **We review our day with the God of our understanding**

Thy will be done, not mine. If we make my will the same as Your will, I will have Serenity & Peace today. Direct my thinking to be divorced from:

  ▷ Self Pity   ▷ Dishonesty   ▷ Self Seeking Motives   ▷ Unfounded Fears

I ask God that my thoughts do not drift into worry, remorse or morbid reflection.

May all my thoughts and actions today be sensitive & tactful without being servile or scraping.

Into Action   -   Fear of the unknown subsides when action is taken.

In thinking about my day ahead, I may be faced with indecision. I may not be able to determine which course to take.   Here I do not struggle alone. I ask God for:

        ▷ An inspiration
        ▷ An intuitive thought or decision, perhaps from his still quiet voice within
        ▷ I relax and take it easy, not forcing my will

**I look to the day ahead to these People, Actions, or Institutions
I will encounter that may bring up character defects:**

▷	**A**	Anger
▷	**R**	Resentment
▷	**SE**	Self-Esteem
▷	**$**	Financial Responsibility
▷	**D/A**	Dreams and Ambitions
▷	**PR**	Personal Relationships
▷	**F**	Fear/Frightened
▷	**L**	Laziness/Sloth
▷	**M**	Materialism
▷	**RT**	Retail Therapy
▷	**S/S**	Selfish/Self Seeking
▷	**DH**	Dishonesty
▷	**D**	Depression/Sad
▷	**J/E**	Jealous/Envy
▷	**P/E**	Pride/Ego
▷	**Fru**	Frustration

In my Thoughts & Prayers today: _____

As I finish my morning meditation and start my day, I offer this prayer to the God of my understanding:

    Here I am. For better or worse, use me as you will. May I follow the guidance of your still small voice. That voice of reason. That voice of another person or my sponsor. Or the collective voice of a home group. Use my strengths and weaknesses in a way useful to others as well as myself. May I have the strength and the courage to follow that still small voice throughout my day. May I behave with grace, sensitivity, tact, consideration and honesty in all situations I encounter this day.

Finally: I remember when I have no clear guidance from God I must go forward quietly along the path of duty.

At the end of the day (10th Step):

I look back at my actions and thoughts during the day just passed, and ask:

     ▷ Was I resentful, selfish, dishonest, or afraid in my words and/or actions?
     ▷ Do I owe anyone an apology?
     ▷ Have I kept something to myself which should have been discussed with another person at once?
     ▷ Was I kind and loving toward all?
     ▷ What could I have done better?
     ▷ I look at my day to be sure I practiced love and tolerance of others as my code.
     ▷ I reviewed my day to see that I have ceased fighting anything or anyone.

I then ask God for what corrective measures should be taken.

The day ahead... the day just passed.   Date:

Date: _____ **We review our day with the God of our understanding**

Thy will be done, not mine. If we make my will the same as Your will, I will have Serenity & Peace today. Direct my thinking to be divorced from:

▷ Self Pity ▷ Dishonesty ▷ Self Seeking Motives ▷ Unfounded Fears

I ask God that my thoughts do not drift into worry, remorse or morbid reflection.

May all my thoughts and actions today be sensitive & tactful without being servile or scraping.

Into Action - Fear of the unknown subsides when action is taken.

In thinking about my day ahead, I may be faced with indecision. I may not be able to determine which course to take. Here I do not struggle alone. I ask God for:

▷ An inspiration
▷ An intuitive thought or decision, perhaps from his still quiet voice within
▷ I relax and take it easy, not forcing my will

**I look to the day ahead to these People, Actions, or Institutions
I will encounter that may bring up character defects:**

_____

_____

_____

_____

_____

_____

_____

_____

_____

▷	**A**	Anger
▷	**R**	Resentment
▷	**SE**	Self-Esteem
▷	**$**	Financial Responsibility
▷	**D/A**	Dreams and Ambitions
▷	**PR**	Personal Relationships
▷	**F**	Fear/Frightened
▷	**L**	Laziness/Sloth
▷	**M**	Materialism
▷	**RT**	Retail Therapy
▷	**S/S**	Selfish/Self Seeking
▷	**DH**	Dishonesty
▷	**D**	Depression/Sad
▷	**J/E**	Jealous/Envy
▷	**P/E**	Pride/Ego
▷	**Fru**	Frustration

In my Thoughts & Prayers today: _____

As I finish my morning meditation and start my day, I offer this prayer to the God of my understanding:

Here I am. For better or worse, use me as you will. May I follow the guidance of your still small voice. That voice of reason. That voice of another person or my sponsor. Or the collective voice of a home group. Use my strengths and weaknesses in a way useful to others as well as myself. May I have the strength and the courage to follow that still small voice throughout my day. May I behave with grace, sensitivity, tact, consideration and honesty in all situations I encounter this day.

Finally: I remember when I have no clear guidance from God I must go forward quietly along the path of duty.

At the end of the day (10th Step):

I look back at my actions and thoughts during the day just passed, and ask:

▷ Was I resentful, selfish, dishonest, or afraid in my words and/or actions?
▷ Do I owe anyone an apology?
▷ Have I kept something to myself which should have been discussed with another person at once?
▷ Was I kind and loving toward all?
▷ What could I have done better?
▷ I look at my day to be sure I practiced love and tolerance of others as my code.
▷ I reviewed my day to see that I have ceased fighting anything or anyone.

I then ask God for what corrective measures should be taken.

Date: _____   **We review our day with the God of our understanding**

Thy will be done, not mine. If we make my will the same as Your will, I will have Serenity & Peace today.
Direct my thinking to be divorced from:

▷   Self Pity   ▷   Dishonesty   ▷   Self Seeking Motives   ▷   Unfounded Fears

I ask God that my thoughts do not drift into worry, remorse or morbid reflection.
May all my thoughts and actions today be sensitive & tactful without being servile or scraping.

Into Action   -   Fear of the unknown subsides when action is taken.

In thinking about my day ahead, I may be faced with indecision. I may not be able to determine which course to take.   Here I do not struggle alone. I ask God for:

> ▷   An inspiration
> ▷   An intuitive thought or decision, perhaps from his still quiet voice within
> ▷   I relax and take it easy, not forcing my will

**I look to the day ahead to these People, Actions, or Institutions
I will encounter that may bring up character defects:**

▷ **A**	Anger
▷ **R**	Resentment
▷ **SE**	Self-Esteem
▷ **$**	Financial Responsibility
▷ **D/A**	Dreams and Ambitions
▷ **PR**	Personal Relationships
▷ **F**	Fear/Frightened
▷ **L**	Laziness/Sloth
▷ **M**	Materialism
▷ **RT**	Retail Therapy
▷ **S/S**	Selfish/Self Seeking
▷ **DH**	Dishonesty
▷ **D**	Depression/Sad
▷ **J/E**	Jealous/Envy
▷ **P/E**	Pride/Ego
▷ **Fru**	Frustration

In my Thoughts & Prayers today: _____

As I finish my morning meditation and start my day, I offer this prayer to the God of my understanding:

> Here I am. For better or worse, use me as you will. May I follow the guidance of your still small voice. That voice of reason. That voice of another person or my sponsor. Or the collective voice of a home group. Use my strengths and weaknesses in a way useful to others as well as myself. May I have the strength and the courage to follow that still small voice throughout my day. May I behave with grace, sensitivity, tact, consideration and honesty in all situations I encounter this day.

Finally: I remember when I have no clear guidance from God I must go forward quietly along the path of duty.

At the end of the day (10th Step):
I look back at my actions and thoughts during the day just passed, and ask:

> ▷   Was I resentful, selfish, dishonest, or afraid in my words and/or actions?
> ▷   Do I owe anyone an apology?
> ▷   Have I kept something to myself which should have been discussed with another person at once?
> ▷   Was I kind and loving toward all?
> ▷   What could I have done better?
> ▷   I look at my day to be sure I practiced love and tolerance of others as my code.
> ▷   I reviewed my day to see that I have ceased fighting anything or anyone.

I then ask God for what corrective measures should be taken.

Date: _____ **We review our day with the God of our understanding**

Thy will be done, not mine. If we make my will the same as Your will, I will have Serenity & Peace today.
Direct my thinking to be divorced from:

  ▷ Self Pity   ▷ Dishonesty   ▷ Self Seeking Motives   ▷ Unfounded Fears

I ask God that my thoughts do not drift into worry, remorse or morbid reflection.
May all my thoughts and actions today be sensitive & tactful without being servile or scraping.

Into Action   -   Fear of the unknown subsides when action is taken.

In thinking about my day ahead, I may be faced with indecision. I may not be able to determine which course to take.   Here I do not struggle alone. I ask God for:

    ▷ An inspiration
    ▷ An intuitive thought or decision, perhaps from his still quiet voice within
    ▷ I relax and take it easy, not forcing my will

**I look to the day ahead to these People, Actions, or Institutions
I will encounter that may bring up character defects:**

▷	**A**	Anger
▷	**R**	Resentment
▷	**SE**	Self-Esteem
▷	**$**	Financial Responsibility
▷	**D/A**	Dreams and Ambitions
▷	**PR**	Personal Relationships
▷	**F**	Fear/Frightened
▷	**L**	Laziness/Sloth
▷	**M**	Materialism
▷	**RT**	Retail Therapy
▷	**S/S**	Selfish/Self Seeking
▷	**DH**	Dishonesty
▷	**D**	Depression/Sad
▷	**J/E**	Jealous/Envy
▷	**P/E**	Pride/Ego
▷	**Fru**	Frustration

In my Thoughts & Prayers today: _____

As I finish my morning meditation and start my day, I offer this prayer to the God of my understanding:

    Here I am. For better or worse, use me as you will. May I follow the guidance of your still small voice. That voice of reason. That voice of another person or my sponsor. Or the collective voice of a home group. Use my strengths and weaknesses in a way useful to others as well as myself. May I have the strength and the courage to follow that still small voice throughout my day. May I behave with grace, sensitivity, tact, consideration and honesty in all situations I encounter this day.

Finally: I remember when I have no clear guidance from God I must go forward quietly along the path of duty.

At the end of the day (10th Step):

I look back at my actions and thoughts during the day just passed, and ask:

    ▷ Was I resentful, selfish, dishonest, or afraid in my words and/or actions?
    ▷ Do I owe anyone an apology?
    ▷ Have I kept something to myself which should have been discussed with another person at once?
    ▷ Was I kind and loving toward all?
    ▷ What could I have done better?
    ▷ I look at my day to be sure I practiced love and tolerance of others as my code.
    ▷ I reviewed my day to see that I have ceased fighting anything or anyone.

I then ask God for what corrective measures should be taken.

The day ahead... the day just passed.   Date:

Date: _____ **We review our day with the God of our understanding**

Thy will be done, not mine. If we make my will the same as Your will, I will have Serenity & Peace today. Direct my thinking to be divorced from:

▷ Self Pity ▷ Dishonesty ▷ Self Seeking Motives ▷ Unfounded Fears

I ask God that my thoughts do not drift into worry, remorse or morbid reflection.

May all my thoughts and actions today be sensitive & tactful without being servile or scraping.

Into Action - Fear of the unknown subsides when action is taken.

In thinking about my day ahead, I may be faced with indecision. I may not be able to determine which course to take. Here I do not struggle alone. I ask God for:

▷ An inspiration
▷ An intuitive thought or decision, perhaps from his still quiet voice within
▷ I relax and take it easy, not forcing my will

I look to the day ahead to these People, Actions, or Institutions I will encounter that may bring up character defects:

▷	**A**	Anger
▷	**R**	Resentment
▷	**SE**	Self-Esteem
▷	**$**	Financial Responsibility
▷	**D/A**	Dreams and Ambitions
▷	**PR**	Personal Relationships
▷	**F**	Fear/Frightened
▷	**L**	Laziness/Sloth
▷	**M**	Materialism
▷	**RT**	Retail Therapy
▷	**S/S**	Selfish/Self Seeking
▷	**DH**	Dishonesty
▷	**D**	Depression/Sad
▷	**J/E**	Jealous/Envy
▷	**P/E**	Pride/Ego
▷	**Fru**	Frustration

In my Thoughts & Prayers today: _____

As I finish my morning meditation and start my day, I offer this prayer to the God of my understanding:

Here I am. For better or worse, use me as you will. May I follow the guidance of your still small voice. That voice of reason. That voice of another person or my sponsor. Or the collective voice of a home group. Use my strengths and weaknesses in a way useful to others as well as myself. May I have the strength and the courage to follow that still small voice throughout my day. May I behave with grace, sensitivity, tact, consideration and honesty in all situations I encounter this day.

Finally: I remember when I have no clear guidance from God I must go forward quietly along the path of duty.

At the end of the day (10th Step):

I look back at my actions and thoughts during the day just passed, and ask:

▷ Was I resentful, selfish, dishonest, or afraid in my words and/or actions?
▷ Do I owe anyone an apology?
▷ Have I kept something to myself which should have been discussed with another person at once?
▷ Was I kind and loving toward all?
▷ What could I have done better?
▷ I look at my day to be sure I practiced love and tolerance of others as my code.
▷ I reviewed my day to see that I have ceased fighting anything or anyone.

I then ask God for what corrective measures should be taken.

The day ahead... the day just passed.   Date:

Date: _____ **We review our day with the God of our understanding**

Thy will be done, not mine. If we make my will the same as Your will, I will have Serenity & Peace today.
Direct my thinking to be divorced from:

▷ Self Pity ▷ Dishonesty ▷ Self Seeking Motives ▷ Unfounded Fears

I ask God that my thoughts do not drift into worry, remorse or morbid reflection.
May all my thoughts and actions today be sensitive & tactful without being servile or scraping.

Into Action - Fear of the unknown subsides when action is taken.

In thinking about my day ahead, I may be faced with indecision. I may not be able to determine which course to take. Here I do not struggle alone. I ask God for:

▷ An inspiration
▷ An intuitive thought or decision, perhaps from his still quiet voice within
▷ I relax and take it easy, not forcing my will

I look to the day ahead to these People, Actions, or Institutions
I will encounter that may bring up character defects:

_____

_____

_____

_____

_____

_____

_____

_____

_____

_____

▷	**A**	Anger
▷	**R**	Resentment
▷	**SE**	Self-Esteem
▷	**$**	Financial Responsibility
▷	**D/A**	Dreams and Ambitions
▷	**PR**	Personal Relationships
▷	**F**	Fear/Frightened
▷	**L**	Laziness/Sloth
▷	**M**	Materialism
▷	**RT**	Retail Therapy
▷	**S/S**	Selfish/Self Seeking
▷	**DH**	Dishonesty
▷	**D**	Depression/Sad
▷	**J/E**	Jealous/Envy
▷	**P/E**	Pride/Ego
▷	**Fru**	Frustration

In my Thoughts & Prayers today: _____

As I finish my morning meditation and start my day, I offer this prayer to the God of my understanding:

Here I am. For better or worse, use me as you will. May I follow the guidance of your still small voice. That voice of reason. That voice of another person or my sponsor. Or the collective voice of a home group. Use my strengths and weaknesses in a way useful to others as well as myself. May I have the strength and the courage to follow that still small voice throughout my day. May I behave with grace, sensitivity, tact, consideration and honesty in all situations I encounter this day.

Finally: I remember when I have no clear guidance from God I must go forward quietly along the path of duty.

At the end of the day (10th Step):

I look back at my actions and thoughts during the day just passed, and ask:

▷ Was I resentful, selfish, dishonest, or afraid in my words and/or actions?
▷ Do I owe anyone an apology?
▷ Have I kept something to myself which should have been discussed with another person at once?
▷ Was I kind and loving toward all?
▷ What could I have done better?
▷ I look at my day to be sure I practiced love and tolerance of others as my code.
▷ I reviewed my day to see that I have ceased fighting anything or anyone.

I then ask God for what corrective measures should be taken.

The day ahead... the day just passed.   Date:

Date: _____ **We review our day with the God of our understanding**

Thy will be done, not mine. If we make my will the same as Your will, I will have Serenity & Peace today.
Direct my thinking to be divorced from:

▷ Self Pity ▷ Dishonesty ▷ Self Seeking Motives ▷ Unfounded Fears

I ask God that my thoughts do not drift into worry, remorse or morbid reflection.
May all my thoughts and actions today be sensitive & tactful without being servile or scraping.

Into Action - Fear of the unknown subsides when action is taken.

In thinking about my day ahead, I may be faced with indecision. I may not be able to determine which course to take. Here I do not struggle alone. I ask God for:

▷ An inspiration
▷ An intuitive thought or decision, perhaps from his still quiet voice within
▷ I relax and take it easy, not forcing my will

**I look to the day ahead to these People, Actions, or Institutions
I will encounter that may bring up character defects:**

▷	**A**	Anger
▷	**R**	Resentment
▷	**SE**	Self-Esteem
▷	**$**	Financial Responsibility
▷	**D/A**	Dreams and Ambitions
▷	**PR**	Personal Relationships
▷	**F**	Fear/Frightened
▷	**L**	Laziness/Sloth
▷	**M**	Materialism
▷	**RT**	Retail Therapy
▷	**S/S**	Selfish/Self Seeking
▷	**DH**	Dishonesty
▷	**D**	Depression/Sad
▷	**J/E**	Jealous/Envy
▷	**P/E**	Pride/Ego
▷	**Fru**	Frustration

In my Thoughts & Prayers today: _____

As I finish my morning meditation and start my day, I offer this prayer to the God of my understanding:

Here I am. For better or worse, use me as you will. May I follow the guidance of your still small voice. That voice of reason. That voice of another person or my sponsor. Or the collective voice of a home group. Use my strengths and weaknesses in a way useful to others as well as myself. May I have the strength and the courage to follow that still small voice throughout my day. May I behave with grace, sensitivity, tact, consideration and honesty in all situations I encounter this day.

Finally: I remember when I have no clear guidance from God I must go forward quietly along the path of duty.

At the end of the day (10th Step):

I look back at my actions and thoughts during the day just passed, and ask:

▷ Was I resentful, selfish, dishonest, or afraid in my words and/or actions?
▷ Do I owe anyone an apology?
▷ Have I kept something to myself which should have been discussed with another person at once?
▷ Was I kind and loving toward all?
▷ What could I have done better?
▷ I look at my day to be sure I practiced love and tolerance of others as my code.
▷ I reviewed my day to see that I have ceased fighting anything or anyone.

I then ask God for what corrective measures should be taken.

Date: _____   **We review our day with the God of our understanding**

Thy will be done, not mine. If we make my will the same as Your will, I will have Serenity & Peace today.
Direct my thinking to be divorced from:
  ▷ Self Pity   ▷ Dishonesty   ▷ Self Seeking Motives   ▷ Unfounded Fears
I ask God that my thoughts do not drift into worry, remorse or morbid reflection.
May all my thoughts and actions today be sensitive & tactful without being servile or scraping.

Into Action   -   Fear of the unknown subsides when action is taken.

In thinking about my day ahead, I may be faced with indecision. I may not be able to determine which course to take.   Here I do not struggle alone. I ask God for:
      ▷ An inspiration
      ▷ An intuitive thought or decision, perhaps from his still quiet voice within
      ▷ I relax and take it easy, not forcing my will

**I look to the day ahead to these People, Actions, or Institutions
I will encounter that may bring up character defects:**

▷	**A**	Anger
▷	**R**	Resentment
▷	**SE**	Self-Esteem
▷	**$**	Financial Responsibility
▷	**D/A**	Dreams and Ambitions
▷	**PR**	Personal Relationships
▷	**F**	Fear/Frightened
▷	**L**	Laziness/Sloth
▷	**M**	Materialism
▷	**RT**	Retail Therapy
▷	**S/S**	Selfish/Self Seeking
▷	**DH**	Dishonesty
▷	**D**	Depression/Sad
▷	**J/E**	Jealous/Envy
▷	**P/E**	Pride/Ego
▷	**Fru**	Frustration

In my Thoughts & Prayers today: _____

As I finish my morning meditation and start my day, I offer this prayer to the God of my understanding:
    Here I am. For better or worse, use me as you will. May I follow the guidance of your still small voice. That voice of reason. That voice of another person or my sponsor. Or the collective voice of a home group. Use my strengths and weaknesses in a way useful to others as well as myself. May I have the strength and the courage to follow that still small voice throughout my day. May I behave with grace, sensitivity, tact, consideration and honesty in all situations I encounter this day.

Finally: I remember when I have no clear guidance from God I must go forward quietly along the path of duty.

At the end of the day (10th Step):

I look back at my actions and thoughts during the day just passed, and ask:
      ▷ Was I resentful, selfish, dishonest, or afraid in my words and/or actions?
      ▷ Do I owe anyone an apology?
      ▷ Have I kept something to myself which should have been discussed with another person at once?
      ▷ Was I kind and loving toward all?
      ▷ What could I have done better?
      ▷ I look at my day to be sure I practiced love and tolerance of others as my code.
      ▷ I reviewed my day to see that I have ceased fighting anything or anyone.

I then ask God for what corrective measures should be taken.

The day ahead... the day just passed.   Date:

Date: _____ **We review our day with the God of our understanding**

Thy will be done, not mine. If we make my will the same as Your will, I will have Serenity & Peace today.
Direct my thinking to be divorced from:

▷ Self Pity ▷ Dishonesty ▷ Self Seeking Motives ▷ Unfounded Fears

I ask God that my thoughts do not drift into worry, remorse or morbid reflection.
May all my thoughts and actions today be sensitive & tactful without being servile or scraping.

Into Action - Fear of the unknown subsides when action is taken.

In thinking about my day ahead, I may be faced with indecision. I may not be able to determine which course to take. Here I do not struggle alone. I ask God for:

▷ An inspiration
▷ An intuitive thought or decision, perhaps from his still quiet voice within
▷ I relax and take it easy, not forcing my will

I look to the day ahead to these People, Actions, or Institutions
I will encounter that may bring up character defects:

_____

▷	**A**	Anger
▷	**R**	Resentment
▷	**SE**	Self-Esteem
▷	**$**	Financial Responsibility
▷	**D/A**	Dreams and Ambitions
▷	**PR**	Personal Relationships
▷	**F**	Fear/Frightened
▷	**L**	Laziness/Sloth
▷	**M**	Materialism
▷	**RT**	Retail Therapy
▷	**S/S**	Selfish/Self Seeking
▷	**DH**	Dishonesty
▷	**D**	Depression/Sad
▷	**J/E**	Jealous/Envy
▷	**P/E**	Pride/Ego
▷	**Fru**	Frustration

In my Thoughts & Prayers today: _____

As I finish my morning meditation and start my day, I offer this prayer to the God of my understanding:

Here I am. For better or worse, use me as you will. May I follow the guidance of your still small voice. That voice of reason. That voice of another person or my sponsor. Or the collective voice of a home group. Use my strengths and weaknesses in a way useful to others as well as myself. May I have the strength and the courage to follow that still small voice throughout my day. May I behave with grace, sensitivity, tact, consideration and honesty in all situations I encounter this day.

Finally: I remember when I have no clear guidance from God I must go forward quietly along the path of duty.

At the end of the day (10th Step):

I look back at my actions and thoughts during the day just passed, and ask:

▷ Was I resentful, selfish, dishonest, or afraid in my words and/or actions?
▷ Do I owe anyone an apology?
▷ Have I kept something to myself which should have been discussed with another person at once?
▷ Was I kind and loving toward all?
▷ What could I have done better?
▷ I look at my day to be sure I practiced love and tolerance of others as my code.
▷ I reviewed my day to see that I have ceased fighting anything or anyone.

I then ask God for what corrective measures should be taken.

The day ahead... the day just passed.   Date:

Date: _____ **We review our day with the God of our understanding**

Thy will be done, not mine. If we make my will the same as Your will, I will have Serenity & Peace today. Direct my thinking to be divorced from:

  ▷ Self Pity ▷ Dishonesty ▷ Self Seeking Motives ▷ Unfounded Fears

I ask God that my thoughts do not drift into worry, remorse or morbid reflection.

May all my thoughts and actions today be sensitive & tactful without being servile or scraping.

Into Action - Fear of the unknown subsides when action is taken.

In thinking about my day ahead, I may be faced with indecision. I may not be able to determine which course to take. Here I do not struggle alone. I ask God for:

  ▷ An inspiration
  ▷ An intuitive thought or decision, perhaps from his still quiet voice within
  ▷ I relax and take it easy, not forcing my will

I look to the day ahead to these People, Actions, or Institutions I will encounter that may bring up character defects:

▷	**A**	Anger
▷	**R**	Resentment
▷	**SE**	Self-Esteem
▷	**$**	Financial Responsibility
▷	**D/A**	Dreams and Ambitions
▷	**PR**	Personal Relationships
▷	**F**	Fear/Frightened
▷	**L**	Laziness/Sloth
▷	**M**	Materialism
▷	**RT**	Retail Therapy
▷	**S/S**	Selfish/Self Seeking
▷	**DH**	Dishonesty
▷	**D**	Depression/Sad
▷	**J/E**	Jealous/Envy
▷	**P/E**	Pride/Ego
▷	**Fru**	Frustration

In my Thoughts & Prayers today: _____

As I finish my morning meditation and start my day, I offer this prayer to the God of my understanding:

  Here I am. For better or worse, use me as you will. May I follow the guidance of your still small voice. That voice of reason. That voice of another person or my sponsor. Or the collective voice of a home group. Use my strengths and weaknesses in a way useful to others as well as myself. May I have the strength and the courage to follow that still small voice throughout my day. May I behave with grace, sensitivity, tact, consideration and honesty in all situations I encounter this day.

Finally: I remember when I have no clear guidance from God I must go forward quietly along the path of duty.

At the end of the day (10th Step):

I look back at my actions and thoughts during the day just passed, and ask:

  ▷ Was I resentful, selfish, dishonest, or afraid in my words and/or actions?
  ▷ Do I owe anyone an apology?
  ▷ Have I kept something to myself which should have been discussed with another person at once?
  ▷ Was I kind and loving toward all?
  ▷ What could I have done better?
  ▷ I look at my day to be sure I practiced love and tolerance of others as my code.
  ▷ I reviewed my day to see that I have ceased fighting anything or anyone.

I then ask God for what corrective measures should be taken.

The day ahead... the day just passed.   Date:

I hope you have found this journal helpful.

If you have any requests, I will gladly make any changes possible, including:
- Additional character defects
- Alternate Higher Powers: God, HP, Goddess or Gus (G.U.S. – Great Universal Spirit)
- Additional blank pages inserted.

Email me at mark@hawkinsm.com or phone (630)372-2069.

(if I don't respond to your email, please give me a call as email occasionally goes to the Spam folder in error)

Made in the USA
Monee, IL
11 September 2023

42543225R00138